The Frontline Leaders

The Challenger Spirit

Advance praise for

The Challenger Spirit

"Reading this book was an experience that was both uncomfortable and inspiring. It helped challenge, reinforce and ignite the Challenger Spirit in me."

Mark Martin, HR Director, Royal Bank of Scotland Insurance.

"I gave this book the 'commute test', i.e. could it keep me captivated on a packed commuter train and the answer was a big YES. The authors capture, explain and beautifully codify the challenger leadership we strive for and (when we are at our best) occasionally glimpse."

Emma Woods, Marketing Director, Pizza Express.

"This work is creative and original. It provides a pragmatic guidance for those who are seeking to create vibrant businesses."

Prof. Hermann Simon, hermann.simon.com.

"A collection of tough challenges that demand the reader to look inwards before acting. It offers many paths through which compassion can permeate organisations and provides thoughtful ways for us to lead into uncertainty. A must read for any Challenger leader."

Craig Bingham, CEO Asia Pacific, Aviva Investors.

"This book refreshed my thinking and reinforced my belief. It challenged me to keep enquiring and searching for different ways to lead and achieve."

Andrew Coull, VP Retail, Everything Everywhere.

"The Challenger Spirit confronts us, not always comfortably, with the necessary tensions required by leaders in order to create a challenger culture around us… It questions, it reframes, it prods, it changes, it illuminates. Hugely stimulating. A book to keep by you."

Adam Morgan, author of Eating the Big Fish and The Pirate Inside.

"I am better for having read this book; it is a bold piece of work."

Kevin Page, General Manager, National Australia Bank.

The Frontline Leaders

The Challenger Spirit

Khurshed Dehnugara
Claire Genkai Breeze

Viva Books

New Delhi | Mumbai | Chennai | Kolkata | Bengaluru | Hyderabad | Kochi | Guwahati

First Indian Edition 2014

VIVA BOOKS PRIVATE LIMITED

- 4737/23 Ansari Road, Daryaganj, New Delhi 110 002
  E-mail: vivadelhi@vivagroupindia.net, Tel. 42242200
- 76, Service Industries, Shirvane, Sector 1, Nerul, Navi Mumbai 400 706
  E-mail: vivamumbai@vivagroupindia.net, Tel. 27721273, 27721274
- Megh Towers, Old No. 307, New No. 165, Poonamallee High Road, Maduravoyal
  Chennai - 600 095 E-mail: vivachennai@vivagroupindia.net, Tel. 23780991, 23780992
- B-103, Jindal Towers, 21/1A/3 Darga Road, Kolkata 700 017
  E-mail: vivakolkata@vivagroupindia.net, Tel. 22836381, 22816713
- 7, Sovereign Park Apartments, 56-58, K. R. Road, Basavanagudi, Bengaluru 560 004
  E-mail: vivabangalore@vivagroupindia.net, Tel. 26607409, 26607410
- 101-102 Mughal Marc Apartments, 3-4-637 to 641, Narayanguda, Hyderabad 500 029
  E-mail: vivahyderabad@vivagroupindia.net, Tel. 27564481, 27564482
- Beevi Towers, First Floor, SRM Road, Kaloor, Kochi 682 018, Kerala
  E-mail: vivakochi@vivagroupindia.net, Tel: 0484-2403055, 2403056
- 232, GNB Road, Beside UCO Bank, Silpukhuri, Guwahati 781 003
  E-mail: vivaguwahati@vivagroupindia.net, Tel: 0361-2666386

www.vivagroupindia.com

Published by arrangement with
LID Publishing
6-8, Underwood Street
London N1 7JQ
UK

ISBN : 978-81-309-2680-3

Published by Vinod Vasishtha for Viva Books Private Limited, 4737/23, Ansari Road, Daryaganj, New Delhi - 110 002.

Printed and bound by Saku Printing House, New Delhi.

For Karin, Ella and Inez.

Contents

Foreword

I didn't mean to read this book.

In fact I refused to take part in the research process when requested. Despite being flattered, I avoid all interviews on the subject of management and leadership as I am shy of being thought of a guru of some kind. Partly this is down to my superstitious nature - it will probably lead to my downfall if I end up as someone to look to! Partly it was down to my distrust of personal histories and the certainties that seem to emerge from them. I suffer from post hoc rationalisation as we all seem to do. Imagining that there was some predefined logic that brought me to where I am now doesn't account for the enormous number of circumstances where old fashioned luck was more influential than any planning or thought. This can have the effect of airbrushing out the often-huge leaps of fortune, accident and unintended consequence that helped along the way.

When sent a copy of the manuscript I ended up reading it from cover to cover very quickly. I found its authors to have generated a work that acknowledged some of my concerns. A number of insights have been culled into a thought provoking piece of writing that is, as far as I know, the best of breed. It will offer many of us comfort… and challenge in knowing that we are not alone.

The writing draws together many interesting observations and creates a story for them which provides an explanation for Challenger behaviours. By drawing a road map that colours in the sort of thought patterns and approaches which identify the Challenger it also provides an incredibly valuable tool for the wannabe Challenger who hasn't quite got it, but who, with a chameleon outlook or attribute, might just be able to make it. So… the book is a great social service and will make many pause to think. I was also encouraged that the writing did not avoid addressing some of the shadowy drives that lead to relentless achievement, restless change and attention seeking behaviour that affect many of our best known Challengers.

With the personal, corporate, societal and environmental tests ahead of us we need many more Challengers in our society, of that I am sure. I know from personal experience just how hard it is to break from the status quo and to keep an organisation from acting like a magnet for what has been done elsewhere. Ultimately I realise that the greatest risk has to be not taking risks, and how many of us can sustain the spirit to keep doing that? I imagine this work will play a part in kick-starting or reinforcing your faith in yourself - that is an honour and a privilege. But also be aware all that the words of others can do is reveal what was there all along and which you did not hear for all the background noise.

In conclusion I have been stimulated, provoked and amused. Considering most other business books are not only badly written, but set themselves up as second rate Bibles this work is to be applauded. It is a Bible for the flawed but willing, and a record of how these vices can be turned into virtues to the benefit of millions of people.

Tim Smit KBE
Co-founder and CEO
Eden Project

Acknowledgements

Challenger Organisations and those leading them often find themselves on the edges of what is accepted as the norm or status quo by the majority, the establishment or the market leader. In my organisational experience I often found myself challenging complacency, narrow mindedness or the proposition that something should only be available to those most privileged. Some of this came from my belonging to a minority in terms of ethnicity or class in my early school, university and employment history. My dear friend, business partner, mentor and co-author Claire Breeze described me as 'arsey' the first time she met me. Nowadays I prefer to think of that state as an (immature) Challenger leader in the making!

Adopting a Challenger position in organisational life inevitably brings with it a degree of relational anxiety. Living with this anxiety has been a part of my life for as long as I can remember. It has moderated over the years and I find myself better able to authentically live with it and thrive in it but that hasn't always been the case.

I strongly believe that if we can allow some personal vulnerability, express ourselves courageously and trust the support around us then we can use our anxiety in a way that benefits our organisations and enriches our lives.

This principle was expressed beautifully by one of our teachers, Professor Ralph Stacey in the following quote. "The true role of a leader of a creative system is not to foresee and take control of its journey, but to contain the anxiety of its members as they operate at the edge of chaos where they are creating and discovering a new future that none could possibly foresee."

Our research interest started with Challenger organisations that were disrupting their market and taking market share from their more established competitors. It subsequently developed as our interest grew in those creating their own Challenger cultures within large Establishment organisations.

At the heart of any successful Challenger organisation are people creating and living in a state of uncertainty and difference of opinion whilst they do their best to disturb and disrupt. Leading an anxious organisation is a life task for a lot of those we have met, worked with and interviewed. A life task for them that begins with learning about themselves and the way their own character manifests in their organisations.

Our clients' experiences have been the lifeblood of this writing, many of them whilst going through particularly challenging times, requiring a step into the unknown together. The quality that distinguished them above all else: they had heart – all of them. Expressed in different ways but their courage is what has inspired us.

There are many other debts of gratitude that run through this writing. To my colleagues at Relume, especially Claire Breeze, Karen Foster, Clare Southall, Jeremy Keeley, Asher Rickayzen, Caryn Vanstone, Roger Taylor and Sam Dunn who have contributed so much to the research, thinking and writing that has become this book. Asher Rickayzen in particular has been the energy and force behind the solid base of individual interviews that form the foundation of this work. But more than this he brought his tenacity and creativity to it whilst the 'it' was still in a formative, foggy and fragile state. In any creative endeavour it takes belief to convince oneself and others of the validity of the work whilst the boulder is being pushed up the hill and Asher provided this for us; he was a true early adopter and without him this book would not exist. Sam Dunn shaped and structured the descriptions for the Challenger patterns of behaviour. He brought a curiosity, discipline and energy that gave us a real breakthrough in how we articulate their essence. Karen Foster's talent for photography and experimentation has adorned our writing with stimulating imagery. Our friend Adam Morgan first wrote about the concept of Challenger Brands from a marketing perspective. If the marketing perspective interests you I strongly recommend reading his revised edition of *Eating The Big Fish*. Adam's consulting work is accessible through www.eatbigfish.com. Brian Harrison was a constant companion and muse through the creative process bringing his decades of advertising experience to the work.

This is a short book. I find nothing more frustrating than struggling through a large tome only to realise at the end that the insights were possible to deliver in a short article. We will be revising this publication as we meet new Challenger leaders who add to our research. More regular updates are available on our Challenger Spirit Blog at www.challengerspirit.relume.co.uk.

Khurshed Dehnugara

****

After 25 years of consulting to organisations, I see myself as a corporate contemplative. In other words I try to allow my Zen Buddhist training to penetrate the mysteries and defences of Establishment organisations for the benefit of the people working within them. Upaya Zen Centre is a radical place of cutting edge learning and deep meditation practice. It is a place of sharp mind and warm heart, embodied by Roshi Joan Halifax and Sensei Beate Stolte my teacher. It may seem like a paradox, but each time I retreat there I feel more passionately that things must change and that there is a real possibility for us to shape that change right now. This book has been informed by Zen teaching and practice and offers the reader some ways into seeing how the modern world of organisations and the ancient wisdom of Buddhism can create a meaningful dialogue with each other. You don't have to be a Buddhist to make some of these approaches work for you.

While I warmly echo all of Khurshed's acknowledgements, I want to point to those influences and sources which are not normally part of the business school reading list, that have woken me up to new ways of thinking and behaving which are not part of the establishment's subtle grip. I think this is part of the Challengers' task; to draw as widely as possible from sources that are free from the constraints of what we are most familiar with.

I have had two lasting influences in my working life. The first came to me at the age of 16 and is 'your work is your love made visible' by Kahlil Gibran. I have never made apology for using that word inside commercial organisations. The second took a little longer to attach itself to me but has been equally powerful. In my forties I read the 5th century Philo's "be kind, for everyone you meet is fighting a great battle". Before reading this I had been sitting with a Board member of a FTSE100 who was stressed, sick and questioning whether he had ever made the kind of difference he went into business to accomplish. He was in pain. It taught me that everyone we work with is actually fighting their own great battle, and that it is possible to extend that view to Establishment organisations themselves. Challengers are at the forefront of a great battle.

Challengers in all spheres of life are truly extraordinary. Over my twenty-five year career I have met more defenders than Challengers, but it is the Challengers I have remembered, have been inspired by and have wanted to introduce to others. What marks these people out is not some higher intellect or greater physical strength. They seem to have conquered two things: one is their fear and the other is an authentic relationship to their true beliefs and values rather than their slogans. I have come to really admire that. What is more, we have to encourage it in people and possibly from a much earlier age than we do currently. It is like seeing the lights go on inside people and that is something you want to follow. Over the years I have worked with some of these leaders long before we coined the term Challenger. However one in particular deserves acknowledgement in this book: Craig Bingham for exemplifying what it means to lead as a Challenger with and through people in such an inspiring way.

I, like all my colleagues in Relume, sit in the thick of all the human and commercial dramas that organisations can produce and I try to think about them deeply and compassionately. At the very same time I am convinced that the only way to change things is to fully engage with them, rather than sniping from the sidelines. This book is inspired by leadership practice, not leadership perfect. This is our work in Relume and we are committed to it.

In gassho.

Claire Genkai Breeze

Introduction

In some ways the Challenger narrative in corporate life started with Avis. In 1963 Avis launched an ad campaign that was very bold and gutsy. Its message was: 'We know we're only the number two rental company. We can't be complacent – we have to try harder. So come on, why not give us a go?' After many years in the red that campaign brought Avis back into the black.[1] This advertising campaign was one that went down in history as one of the best but it couldn't have succeeded without an organisational culture and spirit that backed it up.

We were initially inspired in researching this book by those organisations that developed a spirit that allowed them to take on much larger and better-resourced competitors and win. These Challengers consistently found a way to close the gap between their big ambitions and their traditional resources. This book describes the common patterns of behaviour that we uncovered through our research. At their heart, Challengers find ways of addressing the question 'does it have to be like this?'. This infects their leadership, culture and engagement; encourages a willingness to break with convention and allows them to be more innovative, energetic, contentious and productive.

We set out to investigate 'classic' Challenger stories such as Virgin vs. British Airways, Apple vs. Microsoft, Prêt a Manger vs. Macdonalds, Dyson vs. Hoover, Diesel vs. Levis, Honda vs. Toyota, Amazon vs. Barnes and Noble, Netflix vs. Blockbuster and many others. However, during the process we have also found much insight in those organisations and teams who have recently been much more 'Establishment' in their nature. It is too easy to default to a romantic view of these Establishment organisations as alienating, unfulfilling, monotonous and exploitative. This is not our intention. These businesses have contributed substantially to closing the gap in health and wealth in our society; their leaders want to contribute more. There are many leaders in these businesses that want to rediscover the Challenger spirit that made them successful or create a spirit that will generate a new phase of growth: Diageo, GlaxoSmithKline, Aviva, Royal Bank of Scotland, Hewlett Packard, British Telecom, Nokia, 3M, Intercontinental Hotel Group and many others.

The leaders who have contributed to this work have done their best to bring their ideals into the reality of the complex situations they find themselves in. They have not defaulted to pragmatism or security as a source of avoidance; the domain of the Challenger takes courage. When you are reading this book you would do well to recall that these people are stepping out on behalf of us all. Taking a step to lead from a different place and have that be their signature, publicly recognised in their organisation. How many of us can put our hands up to that?

This book is dedicated to all those doing the work that we have learned from. It is intended to be a source of inspiration, insight and stimulation for would-be Challengers in corporate life and beyond. The work of being a Challenger and developing the organisational spirit is available to us all with sufficient courage, awareness, insight and application. Just as important an audience, however, are those talented, passionate Challengers that are currently losing heart. We want them to read this writing and be encouraged to keep going. To keep going in the face of objection, pessimism or complaint. To keep going in the face of others telling them to stop or to adjust so that they fit in with the rest of the organisation. For many of you the encouragement may come with a realisation that you are a Challenger in an Establishment organisation and that you are not alone.

In absolute terms we want people who lead in Establishment organisations to cause a revolution in the way these companies do their business, relate to their customers and create meaning for their people. To do that they need to cause a revolution within themselves first. To create what they want, they need to undertake the task of practicing a type of leadership that goes against the grain of conventional thinking. So deeply against it that they may find themselves carving a new template for what it means to be themselves. We hope this writing will be a source of assistance. In some places we would like you to realise that you are on the right track, in others maybe to squirm a little as you turn over a page and recognise the Establishment in yourself.

The book has been written with the modern day business reader in mind. Someone short of time, keen to get to the relevant insights without wading through filler and with a desire to put the book down having learned something new that makes a difference to their day to day work. Whilst there is a flow and order to this writing, the book has been structured so that the chapters can be read in isolation. Each chapter following the first focuses on particular inspirations, insights and disciplines that we believe underpin successful Challenger Leaders and their organisations.

The book flows with a beginning and an end on either side of the six Challenger patterns of behaviours that are the core of the work. The foreword, introduction and first chapter set the context for the writing. The last two chapters are a nod to the future and a request to get out there and get on with it! In the middle, the seven chapters on the Challenger patterns follow the same structure: a cover page that gives you some sense of what the pattern is about; insights, stories and stimulation for the Challenger situation that faces you; and a section at the end that is dedicated to your own practice ground, with summaries, the key questions to ponder and a view on what good looks like. It may be worth going to the end of the chapter to see if it will be of interest to you.

The paradox presented in writing about this phenomenon is that it invites us to be 'certain' about uncertainty, something that we don't intend to do. We hope to have provided stimulation, provocation, challenge and thoughtful inquiries with the intention of leaving you with some insight and some questions to ask yourself; to be sometimes less certain, intentionally destabilised in places yet ready to begin, or heartened to continue, the work of creating a Challenger Spirit.

1 Challenger Spirit

"I want to put a ding in the universe."
Steve Jobs Co-Founder & CEO Apple Inc

There is something going on in the successful corporations of our developed economies that makes the timing of this book particularly relevant. Whilst reaching unprecedented size and in some cases profitability, some of these organisations are also, in our opinion, losing the spirit that will be needed to keep them successful. This is evidenced in internal stories of increased bureaucracy, complicated silo based structures, flat productivity, higher R&D spends for lower returns, poor product launches, missed targets, threats from new technologies and increasingly agile small competitors. The external pressures for ever more stringent governance and compliance of these organisations, the rise in successful law suits, the personal culpability of senior corporate officers, and increased PR exposure through digital media channels are all combining to sap the corporate spirit. The question becomes how best to work within this environment and be courageous enough to provide the degree of challenge to the status quo that is required.

In this light there is much to learn from those organisations that are at the heart of this writing – our Challengers. The good news is that if we study what is going on in some of our Challenger leaders, teams, business units and organisations then we see that a strong new competitive spirit inherent in these organisations is expressing itself. It is different from the culture of our Establishment organisations that are still wedded to a metaphor of organisation as a controlled machine, process chart or military hierarchy. It requires us to think differently about our conceptual models of organising, relating, conversing and leading. It requires us to accept challenges to our safe corporate mythology about how to cause substantial and sustained change and renewal.

In addition, many of the talented individuals we have encountered in corporate life are looking for a more enjoyable, stimulating and fulfilling way of conducting their work life. This seems particularly the case with the generation of senior leaders in waiting. Aged between 30 and 45 they are expressing a different world, society and organisational view from that of their predecessors. Their view is more outward looking, globally connected and welcoming of diversity. Critically for the purposes of the story outlined in this book, they are more comfortable making it up as they go along with less of a requirement for certainty about the future. (A certainty that the previous generation of leaders exhausted themselves looking for). The next generation are also much less accepting and more challenging of the status quo. Rather than looking to maintain the status quo they are enthused by challenging it and destabilising it. This holds little fear for them; they have become used to an environment that offers little in the way of security.

Despite that, we have our concerns as to whether the next generation are up to the task. The spirit of an Establishment organisation is insidious; it creeps into your bones within a short time of your working in one. Many of the organisations that attract and employ our brightest talent have a spirit that values security, stability and consistency above most other things. They can be deadening of new possibility – a belief that you can break from the past and create the next organisational future. Despite legions of CEOs striving for, demanding and requesting 'innovation' and 'empowerment', the conditioning of most workforces even at the most senior levels is hard to overcome. They have become so accustomed to doing as they are told, managing the politics and keeping their noses clean, that it is hard to walk through the door even though the CEO is holding it open for them.

The work in developing a Challenger Spirit therefore is as much about the 'Inner work' as it is about the 'Outer work': developing your internal capacities to be a Challenger at the same time as expressing a Challenger Spirit in the team, business unit, organisation or sector that is in need of some destabilisation.

1.1 The Challenger Conversation Beyond Brands

This book takes the concept of Challenger Brands introduced by Adam Morgan in *Eating The Big Fish* and examines further research to generate insight into the spirit behind successful Challenger brands and organisations.

> *While I had embarked upon a book to identify how Challengers use a more intelligent technique, if*

you like, to overcome an opponent's strength, I realised increasingly that what I failed to discuss was the real differentiator, which was something far harder to write about. Spirit.

The Challenger organisations studied typically expressed an ambition beyond the resources available to them. Those examples of organisations that have challenged themselves and their competitors successfully can be a source of inspiration, learning and enjoyment to us all.

This book proposes that Challenger organisations can successfully bridge the gap between their ambition and their resources if they create a particular internal culture and spirit. It utilises insights from successful Challengers and lays out a curriculum for those who aspire to leading Challenger organisations and brands. The core premise is that you have more to learn from Challengers in other markets than you do from copying what the market leader is doing in your own market.[1]

We sold 30% to McDonalds because I was convinced we were doing everything wrong and I was convinced that we would learn from this amazing company with 30,000 branches and I would learn and learn and learn. But unfortunately they just put lawyers and accounting people on our board and we learned very little. This changed towards the last year or so of their ownership... but it was too late. (Julian Metcalfe, Co-founder and CEO Prêt a Manger).

1.2 How Challenger Organisations were Initially Defined

The starting point of this examination was the definition of Challenger brands by market position or ambition and rate of success.[2]

- Challengers are by definition not the market leaders nor are they the niche brands in a market.

- Being a Challenger is not solely about a state of market; being number two or three or four doesn't in itself make you a Challenger. A Challenger is, above all, an ambitious state of mind, rather than a state of market. It is a brand, and a group of leaders behind that brand, whose business ambitions exceed its conventional resources. The organisations we studied did not (and could not) resort to outspending the market leader as a route to success.

- The final criterion for Challengers is that they enjoyed a significant and sustained period of growth through their actions. That is not to say they are still always growing at the same rate, but there is a period of their life that we can learn from. Competitive challenge was typically expressed through innovation in product, distribution channel, strategic positioning or promotional execution. The organisations studied did not grow market share solely through merger or acquisition. The majority didn't benefit from some major technological shift in their favour.

1.3 Research Approach

Part of this research has been conducted through in-depth behavioural event interviews with those leading Challenger Organisations or Establishment Organisations at a senior level. We conducted 50 behavioural event interviews with senior leaders from 40 different organisations. Between them this cohort had been employed at a senior level by over 100 different organisations in their history. Their stories were transcribed and coded for common attributes. The themes were then taken to group conversations with the interview population and others to test them and develop them further. The stories from these interviews have generated much insight, experience and vocabulary.

Ultimately though we have not wanted to write about the Challenger patterns of behaviour purely from someone else telling us about their experience of it. The heart of this work has come from being in the thick of the day-to-day challenges with the executive teams of the organisations we have been advising for ten years.

We don't like being on the outside looking in, we're not academics, and forensically examining leaders, spirit and culture from a distance doesn't do it for us. We are practitioners, committed partners to those organisations that we have been lucky enough to advise over the past ten years. If you spoke to them I hope they would tell you that we, and our colleagues at Relume, live through their experiences with them, holding ourselves responsible for the Challenger patterns of behaviour as much as we hold them responsible. Therefore much of this research has been influenced through 'taking our experience seriously': being constantly in the work and a witness to it, capturing the reflections and insights gathered over ten years, writing them in our learning journals, then looking for helpful themes that support our clients in their work.

1.4 Expanding the Definition of Challenger

The further we researched Challenger Organisations rather than Challenger Brands the more expansive the concepts of Challenger and Establishment became. An ambitious state of mind became as prevalent as market position as a source of Challengers to learn from.

The organisations we have worked with and studied come from three different sources. Our initial investigations polarised organisations into Challengers and the Establishment. We thought it would be interesting to examine those considered to be Challengers by a set of criteria and to understand what could be learned that would benefit Establishment organisations. Of course this was too simplistic and a rich, exciting source of learning came as we talked to more and more people within large Establishment organisations that were keen to develop and express a Challenger Spirit. For many of them this meant being a Challenger on at least two fronts - against Establishment competitors in their market and against Establishment ways of working within their own organisation.

Establishment Organisations

Here is some of what they said to us when asked to describe what was going on in their workplaces. They told us about businesses in crisis. For many of them not a commercial crisis, but certainly a crisis of confidence and leadership. Many of these businesses became successful in the first place through a spirit that was now waning or missing. Despite talented people who had energy, will and technical competence they had difficulty getting any traction on the big changes required if they were to remain competitive.

> *We are in a period of unprecedented challenge in the industry. Of the big companies that exist today one or two may emerge from this as being truly world leading global companies. The choice is to try and lead the pack and be at the forefront of this or to follow others and accept the consequences this brings. We know this but don't really know how to be at the forefront.*
>
> *Our culture is risk averse, bureaucratic, slow and overly analytical - the desire for huge volumes of metrics and management information perpetuates the status quo. There is a significant desire to challenge the market but a lack of creativity or courage to take the leap of faith to something different.*
>
> *Despite all the ambition with a very significant re-brand many within the organisations seem to be reverting to type. We need a different quality of thinking to drive us from the easy 'middle of the road' path, which only leads to mediocrity.*
>
> *We consider ourselves respectful and ethical. We have a strong preference for ideas (diagnosis and design), consultation and consensus, much less for implementation.*
>
> *I would describe us as dictatorial, process centric (over substance), lack of personal accountability,*

complexity is better than simplicity, silo mentality and individual before team.

Lacking in confidence, introspective, stakeholder management driven and burdened by the former glories of past management.

Occasionally ambitious – mostly not. 'What is' is far easier and more comfortable than 'what if'.

I don't think we know how to change anymore, we are trying very hard to become a global, disciplined more structured organisation and at the same time are trying to empower our people and build more accountability across the entire organisation. For many these things appear to be at odds with each other, and whilst they clearly aren't, how we are leading the change suggest that they are.

People are scared to question for clarity for fear of being labelled resistant to change so they keep their heads down and hope to come through the next round of changes unscathed.

A confusing combination of cynical/resistant/ worried and empowered/confident.

We compete in a very dynamic market. We're faced with exciting opportunities for re-invention and growth but our heritage brings baggage than can hold us back against more agile, more entrepreneurial, less corporate competitors.

Challenger Organisations

There was a distinct contrast when talking to those who considered themselves successful Challengers to their competitors or whole market sector. You will note a different tone with little of the crisis of confidence heard from Establishment organisations. Some of the lack of 'discipline' would horrify some Establishment businesses but there was a way of working that was successfully breaking away from the status quo with pace and energy.

> *We are striving to challenge the large incumbent operators by delivering something that is head and shoulders better than the service they are able to offer.*
>
> *Value based, close and trusting teamwork, focus on integrity in all our dealings. We are passionate about delivering a high standard of care to our employees and outstanding delivery to our clients.*
>
> *Our people are warm, genuine and authentic in their desire to help and serve the customer - it is real rather than trained in.*
>
> *We are open, sociable, target driven, adaptable, customer centric, searching and values driven.*
>
> *Change, pace, excitement and anxiety are the words I would use to describe our spirit.*
>
> *We are very much in the driving, "can do" mode akin to a start up company. We have a very open and transparent approach to all activities.*
>
> *We are passionate about our people (not a word on a brand key but genuine commitment). We have a belief in talking – not emailing – striving for genuine engagement. We have a belief in revering and challenging the legacy and traditions of the past and a belief that everyone should have a voice.*

Our engagement scores are incredibly high by any measure and customers continue to tell us that they love our people and it is for that reason they remain our customers. If we have any magic dust, it resides in our people.

Our sales teams are service oriented with up selling and cross sale being a spin off from a conversation rather than the purpose for it.

Challenger Business Units Within Establishment Groups

In many ways this was the most stimulating area of the research. The leaders of these organisations had to find a counter point between one thing and another, Challenger and Establishment. This counter point wasn't stationary, it was constantly moving, flexing and adapting, taking into account both Establishment needs for security and Challenger needs for innovation. They were a source of hope that under the right conditions a Challenger Spirit could be relit or reinvigorated.

The words that come to me are: customer focused, innovative, open, inclusive, engaging, ambitious, analytical, and consultative. But on the flip side, consensus driven and part of a wider group that is risk averse and control focused.

We are in uncharted territory both as a business (joint venture and market changing) and economy and the only way through is by being innovative and nothing short of great at leadership, engagement and communications. Quite different from how we have been in the past.

Entrepreneurial but constrained, creative but could be faster paced, curious, and ambitious. We have a divisional structure that still creates barriers.

Our team has a classical blue chip feeling, has done some excellent work but is still not fast enough and lacks an edge.

Operational, action orientated, young, dynamic but also short term, pragmatic and conformist.

We have a challenger heritage and an internal pride in our brands that could be released to build a giant and iconic business rather that a giant outdated one that we have now.

We are moving from a parental style of relationship riddled with performance issues and a lack of authenticity to a more honest environment, where we regularly confront the brutal truth - both in terms of business issues, people issues and wider strategic issues. In dealing with the good, the bad and the ugly we have become more challenging of our colleagues and ourselves.

We are focused, inquisitive, tenacious within a Group that is dispersed, controlling and gives up easily on novel ideas.

1.5 Developing a New Conversation

This work contributes to a growing body of research that challenges a lot of what has been written in the past about how 'great men' have transformed organisations through a combination of their immense capability, foresight, intellect, skill and determination. Despite being very senior and successful men and women, this is not what our interviewees have chosen in the main to talk about. Challengers don't talk in terms of a 'celebrity CEO'. They were also sceptical of high profile, highly designed and structured, large scale change 'programmes' in their organisations. They were more interested in the inner work of becoming a Challenger – giving up some of the hard wired expectations on them as leaders, and the outer work of becoming a Challenger – the relationships, the conversational approaches, the creation of the most helpful environmental conditions and everyone making it up as they went along. We find this discovery liberating and a relief. There doesn't need to be a reliance on a brilliant few individuals; everyone can get involved, contribute and take responsibility for creating a Challenger organisation.

> *'There's no formula to success. Pixar is driven by 'patterns of behaviour', rather than hard and fast rules. Mike Venturini, Supervising Animator Pixar.*[3]
>
> *When I look back at the change programme that we have just run there were times when I had quite a big 'to do' list. We changed processes and we changed products and we changed marketing. Looking back those were important things but they didn't actually make the biggest difference. As well as a 'to do' list we also had a kind of 'to be' list. Which was about how we related to each other, what we talked about, what we put on our agendas, what we valued as a company, how we behaved with other people in the organisation. That really has been the enduring stuff and the least comfortable stuff for us to do. 'To do' lists were really comfortable, we could tick them off*

and we knew when we had done them. 'To be' lists are harder, you can't measure them you can't tell your boss you have done them quite so easily and they are a real act of faith. (Lee Gladwell, Sales and Marketing Director, Co-operative Financial Services).

ONLY 2 SCHOOL CHILDREN ALLOWED AT A TIME UNLESS ACCOMPANIED BY AN ADULT. THANKYOU
30
FREE SPACE
TOE THE
CAUTION
DO NOT RUN
CAUTION
PUSH
- NO drunkenness, rowdiness or anti social behaviour
- NO loud music
- NO barbeques or fires
- NO camping
- NO fishing without permit
- NO litter
- NO dog fouling - ALL DOGS to be on leads
The Trustees
24 HOUR CCTV IN OPERATION
WODC
NO BALL GAMES
KEEP OFF THE GRASS
for
KEEP FREE
ER
ES

2

Witnessing the Establishment

Waking Ourselves Up

This is about seeing the conventional in your own thinking and that of the organisation around you. It is about understanding where a need for safety is preventing the challenge of outdated habits, norms and routines. It is seeing through what is ingrained in your own thinking and acting. It is about generating and using this insight and sensing where to start. This involves total immersion in what is happening, including an ability to honour and learn from the past, whilst understanding what keeps you and the people around you attached to the status quo. It is being able to both immerse yourself in the present and stand back and see things differently at the same time.

This business tends to like people who are very operational and highly target focused. It's a big machine; I suppose you need a lot of uniformity if you are going to employ this many people. It would be hard to run if you didn't have rigorous processes. The problem is you don't tend to learn from many others because everyone has a similar style, there isn't a lot of variety. It's hard if you want to do things differently and after a while you find that you stop asking. I have been here twelve years, I used to get angry about it for the first two years and then I stopped asking. (Anonymous Director, British Telecom.)

When I joined HP a long time ago I can remember how angry I was about the overriding assumption that things are always done this (the HP) way because they always have been and alternative views were ignored or squashed. I can remember venting my spleen on many occasions because it felt so frustrating to be locked in a world that was completely self-referencing when I felt I had so much more variety that I could offer. I ended up working mainly on interim projects to fill gaps before the major projects delivered (which of course they rarely did) where there was more opportunity for experimentation. It was stifling. (Anonymous Director, Hewlett Packard.)

Challengers have learned that at all times they need some connection to an activity that encourages new life. They generate more vibrant places to work as a consequence. That is not to say that they are always following a growth agenda but that there is somewhere in the business that keeps even a small part of growth and innovation alive. And because they are committed to it they see that it won't be given up on easily or drown in the sea of sacrifices. They are thinking, pushing and inquiring. Where are we allowing ourselves to be uncertain? What do we still need to learn? What are we doing that is bringing some new life to our organisation? Where do we want to generate some instability in the market? How do we want to take advantage of instability that already exists? How are we making the most of the energy this generates? What are we encouraging our organisation to get excited about? Where are we trapped by our own success?

Witnessing the Establishment is a critical precursor to any act of being a Challenger. To bear witness requires some determination, some letting go and plenty of inner work. It is a skill underpinned by a courageous attitude. It is an attempt to truly see what is being ignored, avoided, causing antagonism or too easily agreed to. Witnessing the Establishment is to experience the full effect of your organisation on everyone that touches it, including yourself. In doing so you experience what it does to your intellect, your heart, your motivation, your energy, your will to change things, your hope and ambition.

2.1 An Addiction to Stability and Safety

> *The question we don't seem to ask ourselves is 'what is the risk of not failing?' (Louise Mountain, BBC Worldwide.)*

For the purposes of this work we are going to polarise organisations and make the antithesis of the Challenger organisation the Establishment organisation. We know as discussed in the last chapter that the real world is not that simple but we think it helpful to make this simple distinction. The Establishment organisation exposes itself to obsolescence, decay and competitive threat when it prefers security and more of the same. Instinctively many leaders of establishment organisations know this but find it difficult to do anything meaningful about it.

> *When Peter Voser took over in 2009 as CEO of Royal Dutch Shell, the world's market leading oil company, he sent a companywide memo part of which complained that the organisational culture was "too consensus-oriented".*

The myth of a safe and certain organisation that continues to win based on past successes is a seductive one. Many of us work in organisational environments that are obsessed with the elimination of any possible risk. We want to believe that if we keep doing what worked for us in the past that we will be okay. We develop very strong attachments to the status quo and even stronger attachments to measuring the status quo. Through this mechanism we reinforce to ourselves why it is still 'the right thing to be doing', paralysing ourselves towards rigidity, avoiding the critical role that being uncertain has to play in our creative processes. Leaders who need to play safe and look good in conventional terms are unlikely to be those who become successful Challengers.

> *In late 2007... H-P started promoting a warranty for its switches that provides free upgrades and support. Under Cisco's new structure, a decision about how to respond to H-P's offering was delayed as it worked its way through multiple committees, these people said. Cisco didn't match H-P's promotion until April 2009, and during that*

period, Cisco's market share fell. (John Chambers, CEO, Cisco).[1]

Perfect adaptation to the present makes it much more difficult to adapt to the future when the environment changes. When the game changes for the Establishment organisation because of a Challenger competitor's action, or a shift in the competitive environment, there is no longer enough creative capacity or capability in the organisation to respond with pace. Thinking has become stale and the conversation has become ossified.

The organisation is trapped by conversations about what it knows and is unable to create new ones about what it doesn't know. There has been less interest in *what* is being done, more interest in improving the efficiency of it.

Establishment organisations are often exposed to Challengers when their culture becomes more adept at playing safe than disrupting outdated norms and routines. In many cases the Challenger has been more adept than the Establishment organisation at thriving on uncertainty, diversity of opinion and the associated cultural anxiety.

2.2 The 4 As: Establishment Blindfolds

What drives me crazy? The politics in the corporate world. Most people have to accept it and they do it. But it is a complete waste of energy – you can't say what you want to say when you want to say it. Even in my organisation that causes me more worry and heartbreak and CEO than anything else. (Julian Metcalfe, Co-founder and CEO, Prêt a Manger.)

The work of Witnessing The Establishment begins with first recognising where you are unhelpfully accepting or reinforcing the status quo. In our experiences we have noticed some subtle ways in which Establishment leaders and leadership teams stop themselves exploring uncharted territory and allowing the Challenger Spirit to thrive. We have called these four blindfolds the four As: Arrogance, Avoidance, Agreement and Antagonism.

Arrogance

The success that has built many Establishment organisations often brings with it a degree of arrogance. Having a belief that you are the best, untouchable, not to be questioned, leaves you vulnerable to threats from your competition. Not least because avoidance of meaningful conversations about your vulnerability removes a healthy paranoia that successful organisations have had at their heart.

Arrogance is sometimes expressed through the brute strength that comes with size overtaking the competitive brilliance that will have helped a company to grow in the first place. Sometimes the first stage of a death spiral is an organisation throwing its weight around to crush competitors as opposed to out smarting them in the eyes of the consumer. They lose their thought leadership position to the Challenger and start fulfilling some of the more negative stereotypes that come with their size and success.

Another aspect of size is the increased structure, hierarchy, fragmentation and silo mentality that comes with it.

Sony should never have lost territory to Apple with the iPod. It was perfectly positioned to continue to own portable music as a category from its heritage with the Sony Walkman, through portable disc players and the mini-disc. On top of all these assets it also owned a publishing company Sony Music and had a big presence in music, something that Apple was lacking.

The arrogance of the Establishment player expressed itself partly through their insistence to continue with the development of analog technologies and not commit to digital.

The fragmentation of the business evidenced itself through the fact that even though they launched the first digital music player two years before Apple, they launched two, both flawed, each produced by a different silo in the business. On top of this was a third silo in the form of Sony Music who did not commit to the new technologies for fears over music piracy.[2]

Success and size also limits the chances of new breakthroughs bubbling up from your workforce as the hierarchy ends up suffocating challenging new ideas and ways of working. A concern for Establishment organisations is the effect their culture may be having on the creative Challengers in their own workforce.

The mythology that surrounds the enterprise software organisation SAP suggests that it was founded by challenger individuals within the ranks at IBM who could not get the support for their ideas to thrive in the IBM culture at the time. All the contracts that SAP has subsequently won could have been IBM's in another scenario.

Taking off the Arrogance blindfold leaves you able to witness where your past success has become in some way self limiting. It allows you to see again with new eyes your competitive landscape and to begin asking uncomfortable questions of yourself and others.

Avoidance

An easy way to play safe and look good is just to steer clear of any of the Challenger conversations that you know are going to get messy.

A typical form of avoidance commonly practiced is to refer difficult conversations and choices up to the top team, expecting them to sort them out for you. Then when the decision comes down from on high you can implement it safe in the knowledge that someone else has sanctioned it. This form of avoidance has particularly far reaching consequences for the culture of an organisation. It learns that empowerment is limited, that conflict is resolved at the top of the organisation, that it is better to be safe than courageous.

You can also use the complexity of an organisation to hide behind. Let's face it, things are so fragmented, siloed and fast moving at present that most organisations can have internally conflicting positions taken on strategy or implementation and it not be noticed for a long time.

The most subtle form of avoidance is to collude with the current organisational culture or preference for the way things are done, despite knowing that leadership of a Challenger organisation often requires one to step outside and challenge the old habits in place.

When you take this blindfold off you are able to see the damage that avoidance causes and be more honest with yourself and others about where courage has been missing.

Agreement

In the context of Establishment organisations easy agreement is another way to reduce anxiety and play safe. Agreement in these terms can mean finding a way to progress by agreeing at a level of detail rather than of principle, content rather than context. For example, it is possible to agree that a new positioning is needed for a brand without really working through the implications for whether the organisation is sales led or brand led. It is possible to keep agreeing that an organisation transforms without paying attention to how individuals will need to transform. It is possible to agree big revenue generating strategies for the future without paying attention to the sacrifices they will require in the current financial year. It is possible to agree that creating a Challenger culture is a key strategic theme in the organisation without really working through the implications of what this means for the Executive Team.

Agreement feels like progress but often the agreement has been reached through reducing complex dilemmas to simple problems that can have a right/wrong solution. When such an agreement is put in place, leaders tend to breathe a sigh of relief, thinking that is another tick against the list, only for the agreement to unravel when it is tested against the complexities of daily organisational life. The unravelling often happens at some distance with the leaders' teams struggling first and foremost. Easy agreement becomes a form of abdicating leadership responsibility.

The response to agreements unravelling is usually the exertion of increased levels of control. Leadership focus ends up on applying your authority, rather than facilitating a more useful conversation in the organisation. So we create a culture dependent on high levels of agreement and low levels of uncertainty. Not the natural territory of a Challenger organisation.

When this blindfold is removed leaders are better able to engage with and make meaning from the complex connections and interdependencies in their organisations. They are more open to and adept at dealing with diversity of opinion and uncertainty of action.

Antagonism

Another subtle way of reducing anxiety and looking good is to take an antagonistic position in response to the proposals put forward for leading a Challenger organisation.

As leaders growing up in the organisations of the past 20 years, we have learned to admire those that can form a strong view and then attach themselves to it in an unyielding way. This 'strong leader' model is often mythologized through stories of how this determination, stubbornness and consistency generated a breakthrough.

Inevitably if one position is taken up strongly by a Challenger leader, then someone else will soon support the other pole and the antagonism is in play. If you respond with more antagonism then this has far reaching effects for trust, transparency and fragmentation of effort. In most organisations we have worked with, this way of operating leads to a lot of leadership energy being wasted on competitive and defensive positions being taken up. Before you know it, whole organisational structures have been built in response to something that was motivated by the politics of power rather than doing the right thing.

> *Given the scale of strategic and structural change going on inside most companies, one of the most important challenges facing CEOs is to communicate that change internally. Internal communication to secure internal alignment is, perhaps, a polite way of putting it. Probably the biggest block to progress for our clients – and perhaps ourselves – is internal politics. Turf, territory and ego prevent productive change. If the chairmen or CEOs of our clients saw what we saw, they would be horrified. If they and we devoted 50% of the time that they or we spent on internal politics on the consumer, client or competition, they and we would be considerably more successful. (Sir Martin Sorrell.)*[3]

Successful leadership of a Challenger involves accepting that there will be sources of antagonism expressed towards your leadership and knowing how to navigate them so that you don't end up very stuck in an exhausting and unproductive dynamic.

Taking this blindfold off also allows us to acknowledge how we are contributing to the dynamic, helps us move away from absolutes, making ourselves always right and the other party always wrong.

Taking the blindfolds off is hard. We have a lot of compassion for those people in organisations that default to the 4 As. The environment they are working in has never been more uncomfortable than it is now and they are doing their best to navigate it successfully. If Challengers can raise consciousness of this limiting style of leadership, we have some hope of being able to change it. More than ever, we need organisational leaders who are willing to express themselves courageously and authentically without looking good, personal ego and security being their primary concern.

2.3 The Death Spiral

The 4 As interest us in particular because we think they are the precursor to further deterioration in organisational performance – early indicators that something is amiss. If not dealt with they can tip the culture into what we describe as a death spiral. The death spiral is not characterised by a mass panic but a steady deterioration in the capability of the organisation to thrive in the uncertainty of the market place. Over time internal belief deteriorates, energy dips, external confidence is lost, there is an over-checking of the choices being made and the business loses its agility. In the middle of this is the time when Establishment businesses are most vulnerable to competitive threat from a Challenger.

In an Establishment organisation that is tipping into the spiral the cultural environment starts to feel highly constrained, the number of strategic choices available are reduced. There is an over emphasis on the back end of the business and sacrificing activity, headcount, promotional plans becomes addictive as a way of meeting the profit targets. There is a slowing down of and ultimately a paralysis of decision-making. Politically individuals and teams have a pre-occupation with looking good. Personal reputations start driving the agenda and it becomes harder for teams to do what is needed because so much time is put into managing the measures and the stakeholders. If you are in the middle of this you are often exhausted and even the most positive of people see little real hope in the future.

> *Yahoo has entered this spiral and is struggling hard to come out of it. It still has an enormous size and is still second in the market of search related advertising after being pushed into that position by the Challenger Google. But it has lost substantial market share as the online audience fragments to numerous alternative Challengers such as Facebook. This is a peculiar fate for an organisation that grew revenues (including acquisitions) at an average of 55% annually from 2001 to 2006.*

The death spiral may sound dramatic in terms of language but having worked inside many of these organisations the energy does feel 'dead'. It is reflected in the kinds of conversations that are had, the way people move, the tone of their voices, the level of creativity they can access.

The spiral is a useful image as the further into it you progress the harder it is to pull yourself out. This is particularly the case when something is deemed to have 'failed' in the eyes of the organisational stakeholders - customers, shareholders, staff or regulators. When you are in a death spiral, suffering an initial failure makes the second failure more likely, which makes a third more likely and so on.

> *I mean right now their own cabin crews are destroying British Airways. A strong brand that*

gets attacked by itself - the internal perception is that they don't treat their staff right and the staff bites back. A danger for most establishment organisations, almost like a virus that eats the organisation from the inside. (Chris Moss, ex CMO, Virgin Airlines.)

Whenever our leaders are damaged in this way not only does it decrease their current performance but also their strength and dexterity to respond to the next challenge which is never too far away.

Mr. Norman, the former head of Asda, who joined ITV at the turn of the year, said: "We want and need to be Europe's fastest changing media company." Mr Crozier, who arrived from Royal Mail several months later, said the transformation plan would help shape "a lean business that creates world class content executed over multiple platforms, which can also be sold globally". The group also took a swipe at previous management, saying that 90 per cent of underperformance over the past ten years had been self-inflicted.[4]

It is not too difficult to imagine how those businesses that were not able to respond enough to a Challenger's threat will have been dominated by the 4 As in action: too wedded to their past through avoidance, agreement or antagonism to see the scale and speed of what was approaching.

2.4 Towards Safe Uncertainty

Pulling a business out of a spiral is hard work but some of those we have interviewed and worked with have managed to do so. Some of their stories have informed the Challenger credos outlined in the following chapters.

> *I was just about delivering on plan but I felt like I was failing. I had never failed at anything before in my life, I tried everything I knew and it didn't make any difference. It was a personal crisis for me. I decided that with our new strategy I would pull the big lever and work on the leadership, culture and spirit of the division. (Stuart Fletcher, President of International, Diageo.)*

> *A lot of big companies come with a lot of heritage, a lot of pride in their brands, you have got people who are committed and work hard. That is not enough for what we are talking about. We keep doing the same things we have always done, sometimes working into the middle of the night and we are not going anywhere. Large incumbent businesses that know that what they are currently doing is dying, their position is dying. Being a new Challenger rising from a small size is brilliant but now the exciting question for me is 'is it possible for a giant company to become a Giant Challenger?' (Mark Martin, HR Director, Royal Bank of Scotland Insurance.)*

At the heart of the Challenger Spirit is a belief in the paradoxical sounding mindset of safe uncertainty.[5] We don't underestimate the difficulty of adopting this position. Our Establishment organisations have been built since the industrial revolution on the premise that security only comes through certainty. This is reflected in everything about the way these organisations manifest – their symbols, artefacts, structures, processes, mindsets, relationships and behaviours.

From the time I left IBM I have never been in a business where we could keep up with the market leader in terms of spend. I think not having the big budget that the number one does is a better place to be, it forces you to look harder at the reality of the customer experience rather than just splash out on advertising and telling people how great you are. It forces you to focus your scarce resources on what matters to the customer. If you have all the resources you need it can make you a bit fat, dumb and happy. Not having everything you want keeps you sharp. You just kind of move on in Amazon, there is not a great deal of back patting, we have restlessness for the next thing rather than the last thing. (Brian McBride, CEO, Amazon UK.)

Many of the complaints that leaders have about their Establishment organisations are rooted in the very way these same organisations are led. It is within our power to change the spirit of an organisation so that it better reflects the spirit of a Challenger but first we have to witness the Establishment practices that are going on in ourselves and in the environments we are creating.

- Believing that everything can be managed as separate parts of a machine. Paying little attention to the environment that exists outside of our organisation, being myopic in our internal focus.
- Lacking curiosity in the possibilities that may exist outside of our sequential, linear, cause and effect frame of reference.
- Over relying on centralised decision making, command and control, bureaucracy and policies to provide direction.

- Accepting and ignoring fragmented relationships, turf wars, silos, overlaps and duplications.
- Solving conflicts through linear either/or thinking, avoiding paradox, clinging to our old successful formulae for success.
- Allowing rhetoric and wanting to look good to have as much currency as real, messy, authentic leadership in action.
- Undermining the need for experimentation and learning through an implicit emphasis on not making a mistake.

One of the first things we did was to employ a manager for the first shop who had experience from elsewhere. After two years of listening to this manager we stopped and did it our own way. He just didn't have the courage to try things differently to what he had done before. (Julian Metcalfe, Co-founder and CEO, Prêt a Manger.)

Challenger Spirit is rooted in being able to challenge norms, conventions and habits both inside ourselves and in the environments that we lead. Before we can challenge them we have to be able to see them clearly and with the best interests of the organisation at heart.

The Practice Ground

We once sat around the board table of a very well known organisation that had commissioned some internal research to find out what was going on in the organisation. It was a costly and lengthy process. As the findings were revealed the dominant discourse around that table was not "what is this revealing to us?" but " how can we prove you wrong?" These leaders were not challengers, they were defenders; they had no interest in witnessing their own organisation and they wanted to defend it from insight that they viewed as an attack.

It is hard to see things as they really are. Most of the time we witness anything our view of reality bends what we see to fit more easily with our internal landscape. Through our Challenger work we help people to access a number of skills that are based in mindfulness training and supported by some extraordinary findings emerging from the field of neuroscience.

The problem for most of us leading in organisations is that we do not see our thinking as habitual because our mind is transparent to us. Conventionally we think of the word transparent in an organisational context as a good thing. Here the neuroscientists are using the term transparent to point to something we cannot see, and because we have not trained our minds to see it, we cannot witness things as they are - a whole area of awareness is not available to us.

From the perspective of the inner establishment, the inner landscape that each of us has developed over years has become so familiar to us that we no longer see it as an idiosyncratic response to the world. By encouraging leaders to learn the skills of intentional attention[6] they are discovering a tool that is central to the ability to Witness the Establishment.

When the leaders that we work with are helped to bring intentional attention to their ways of seeing and thinking about their organisational life, their own mental activity becomes opaque. In other words for the first time, leaders can actually experience what they are thinking, seeing, feeling as a product of their mind. They become a witness to themselves in action and to the wider field in which they are operating. They achieve meta-awareness; meta-cognition or what is more commonly referred to right now as mindfulness.

This is the first and most profound step to achieving mastery of the Witnessing the Establishment pattern of behaviour. Without the movement from transparent to opaque no leader can do anything other than duplicate what they think they already know. If you multiply this by enough powerful leaders in an organisation you see the birth of Establishment culture. However with meta-awareness, the power of mindfulness starts to dissolve the Establishment influence of habit, accepted norms and blind spots. It is the turning point in a leader's ability to liberate their own inner Establishment and that of others.

When leaders develop the skill of meta awareness, not simply the theoretical knowledge about it, their whole leadership discourse, their ways of speaking and relating begin to change. The field of neuroscience is revealing how much we can alter our capacity to become a true Challenger by intentionally attending to our minds. This practice ground is the key to unlock mastery of the other patterns.

Getting Stuck In

Inner Work

- How much do you feel you owe the current establishment for your success?
- Since working here what have you become less sensitised to?
- What are you avoiding, knowing that if you really see it you will have to do something?
- What aspects or issues that others complain about in your organisation do you have little time for?
- What are the subtle things you notice in yourself that are an indication of something deeper?

Outer Work

- How could you immerse yourself and your team in really experiencing the organisation from the perspective of staff, customers, associates etc?
- How can you encourage your team to notice more of what is going on in the organisation and to share what they are learning?
- Which areas are the Challenger bright spots and what happens there?
- Which areas are most demonstrative of the Establishment shadow? What happens there and what effect is it having?
- Which conversations do you believe are off limits and why?

Your Notes, Insights and Scribbles

What Good Looks Like

Seeing past conventional wisdom and confronting conformity.

- Shows a curiosity about the future and new possibilities.
- Sees what is keeping the organisation attached to the past.
- Realises and articulates self limiting beliefs that need to change.
- Sees what the self and the organisation need to move away from.
- Is not limited by the accepted way of thinking about issues.
- Sees beyond what was and is to what could be.

Deep insight that something needs to change.

- Is able to become immersed in a situation and get beneath the surface of issues.
- Understands the internal and external organisational context and how they fit together.
- Brings insight from previous experiences but is not limited by them.
- Is able to emerge from the detail of the situation and provide an objective insight into what is happening.
- Is able to understand issues in terms of relationships, behaviours, structures and processes.

Understanding the consequences of inaction.

- Understands and articulates the consequences of staying the same.

- Understands and articulates the consequences of ignoring the signals that something needs to change.
- Sees the importance of examining anxieties about the future.
- Sees the importance of examining what is making the organisation anxious about the future.

Knowing where to start, where not to and amplifying bright spots in the organisation.

- Shows the insight and creativity to see how to unfreeze the team / organisation.
- Is able to identify and leverage points of entry.
- Thinks broadly about multiple complex agendas.
- Understands the likely points of resistance and scepticism.
- Understands where the real power is in the team / organisation.
- Is able to see what has caused false starts in the past.
- Understands the readiness for change.
- Looks for the parts of the team / organisation where there is the most potential for change or where the desired future is already in play.
- Is able to assess the way forward in complex situations.
- Sees where disturbance is needed in the organisation to change things.

3

Purposeful Instability

Rocking The Boat

This is about destabilising things in order to allow something new to emerge, applying ongoing moderate disturbance that encourages contention, creativity and experimentation. It is relishing the energy that is generated from upsetting the equilibrium and understanding how this can liberate others. It is helping others to understand how destabilising things can catalyse change and helping them to manage their reactions. It requires courage and confidence in thought and action. It is seeing and allowing possibilities to emerge by creating ambiguity, not being daunted by the uncertainty this creates and having the patience not to close things down before value is harvested. It requires high levels of self and organisational awareness in order to be able to connect with others and use anxiety in a creative way.

Our goal is to be destructive but in the cause of making the world a better place. (Attributed to the co-founders of Skype.)

3.1 The Disturbance Matrix

The overriding pull of the Establishment organisation's spirit is towards maximum certainty, super efficiency and minimum disturbance. In contrast, Purposeful Instability is the pattern at the heart of any successful Challenger. The nature of the Challenger is one that pulls towards ongoing moderate disturbance, putting them in the territory marked out by experimentation, creativity, contention and learning. This is all in the service of an organisational spirit that will enable significant acts of transformation. The process is inevitably anxiety provoking so a service that Challenger organisations need from their leaders is ongoing, confidence-building support in the face of pressures to conform and avoid the new and the difficult.

Figure 3.1 The Disturbance Matrix.

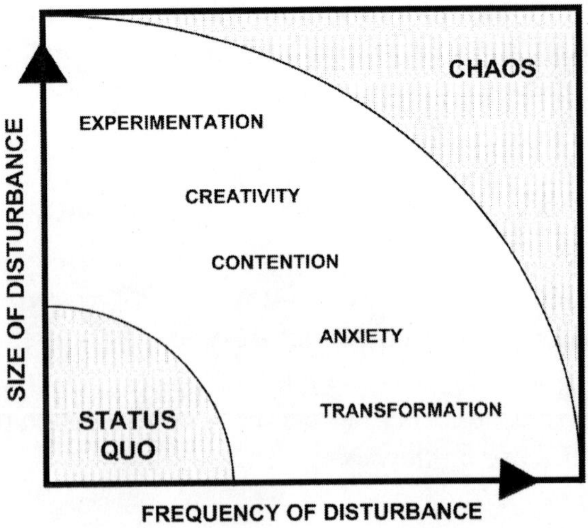

Our competitors have done so brilliantly at being efficient, they have nothing left in their spirit. It's a reason why we feel confident in our ability to succeed against them. You can feel it, when you walk into a place that demands that much certainty and agreement you can feel it in the air, little spirit, laughter, relationship or individualism. Everyone you speak to has the same script. (Graham Neale, SVP Nutritional Healthcare Future Group, GlaxoSmithKline.)

It is the intention of a successful Challenger to create waves organisationally by causing ongoing moderate levels of disturbance. They are metaphorically throwing boulders into still waters and then having to learn how to surf the waves they themselves have generated. For a Challenger these waves are a positive sign, a signal of hope that they are causing enough disturbance to break from the past, to challenge the old norms and routines.

It was the first national campaign that Costa had executed, this was about agitation, the first time any coffee brand had advertised nationally in the UK, to be so confident and so aggressive against our competition was quite a shock to the category.

"Seven out of Ten" was a massive change of direction for Whitbread. Whitbread is traditionally a conservative place not renowned for taking risks, a very high performing business based on small incremental steps. Costa has brought a campaign that was very aggressive, targeting a fearsome large competitor, it was a quantum shift from the way things had been done. So yes

there was an awful lot of lobbying, explanation, negotiation at a senior level to get that campaign away. (Jim Slater, Marketing Director, Costa Coffee.)

At the same time, whilst the Challengers we have researched are bold in their actions, they are also not reckless in their custodianship of their organisations.

> *"'Screw it let's do it' are my five favourite words as an entrepreneur. They so often cut through all the dithering in business. That said, "protecting the downside" are my three other favourite words. One needs to be sure before one can be bold, try new things and still afford the cost if the project doesn't work out." (Sir Richard Branson, Chairman, Virgin Group.)*[1]
>
> *The risks we have taken have been well considered. We have a good mixture of born risk takers and those that are inclined to apply the brakes. Costa is not going to blow up as a result. (Jim Slater, Marketing Director, Costa Coffee.)*

This middle ground in the Disturbance Matrix of moderate, not too low, not too high a level of disturbance is a difficult one to stand in for long periods of time. There are always going to be competing pulls on your energy. A pull for more creativity and challenge always being moderated by a pull for less anxiety and more control.

> *The impact on the leadership team is significant; they need to hold the tension and that can feel very uncomfortable at times. On one hand you want to enable people around you to do their best*

work under increasingly uncertain circumstances on the other you are expected to report 'order' in a way that is detached from the reality of running the business – it's comical really. It's easy to underestimate how difficult it is to sit amongst these tensions.

The demands for predictability and order, recorded in multiple templates, often have nothing to do with the way you are running the business. The further towards chaos you are the more it provokes anxiety in yourself and your team, sapping everyone of his or her energy as they try and hold the tension between the chaos they are experiencing and the order they are reporting! (Chris Harley-Martin, VP Global Business Development, GlaxoSmithKline.)

Those creating a Challenger culture will need to examine their own relationships to issues of image, power, potency, control, security, surprise, vulnerability, trust, and fear if they are to successfully lead their organisations into this territory of ongoing moderate disturbance. This theme is picked up in the remaining Challenger patterns of behaviour.

One of the most important parts of leading people in a Challenger is that they have a sense of their own inner security and confidence so that they are able to take risks, create disturbance and deal with difficult situations. The extent of the strength of their inner core determines the ability to take those steps and really jump into the change. (Emma Krygler, Director of Engagement, Everything Everywhere.)

3.2 Destabilising Establishment Competitors

Putting a moderate level and moderate frequency of disturbance into the market destabilises Establishment organisations and benefits Challenger organisations. This is helpful if you are a Challenger organisation competing with an Establishment organisation.

> *Warburtons has succeeded in protecting its profit margins after refusing to make own-brand bread for supermarkets. That strategy helped it become the first of the big bakers to break through the £1-a-loaf barrier. The company has been quiet about its success. Warburton said last year: "It's a success story that we have not shouted about from the rooftops. Having a bit of a chip on our shoulder is a good thing. We've tried to use our flat-cap-and-whippet chip in a positive way. So we've laughed at ourselves for being simple northern folk, but it can be quite galvanising".*[2]

Challenger organisations and their leaders are more likely to fail when they imitate rather than disturb their Establishment competitors. They fail when they default to what is already known to be successful, when they stick to standard practices and what the consumer is currently buying the most of, and compete only according to the field that the market leader has initiated. This is usually all done in the interests of security and continuing to look good. Leaders don't tend to get sacked for doing more of what is successful elsewhere.

> *There was lots of activity and commitment but when nothing is changing at the core then*

you know that simply applying your energy is not enough. (Juan Pemberton, Director Of Leadership, RBS Insurance.)

If the Challenger's products or services are truly to be breakthrough innovations that challenge the market, they may even be derided and ridiculed by their Establishment competitors whose continued success depends on maintaining a high level of certainty and continuity.

In the mid 90's Orange launched its Orange Value Promise, it was a brilliantly simple idea. It consisted of offering all their competitors price plans on the Orange network so there was no need for any existing or prospective customers to go anywhere else. It was massively successful and allowed them to dramatically increase their market share.

I remember the weekly commercial review meetings when we pored over our disappointing sales figures and explained them by the impact of the Orange Value Promise. Despite knowing what the problem was we found it very difficult to know how to respond. We spent a long time talking about it, analysing it, denying that it could be made to work and getting angry that it did work but most of the time we were frozen by uncertainty and did nothing (except lose market share).

Periodically we would invest time and energy in considering legal action; looking at building the capability ourselves so that we could copy what they were doing; making ourselves feel better by looking for data to suggest that their customers were unhappy with some element of the Orange service. In the end we just wasted a lot of time and remained stuck in the web of our own indecision. (Vodafone Director.)

It is so much more difficult to know how to respond to a Challenger action when you have something to lose because there is more at stake both financially and emotionally. The decision of whether to take the challenge full on and respond in an overt way or whether to sit it out and hope that the challenge withers away is a difficult one. By responding to the challenge you are often in the position of having to cannibalise your own growth, revenue, share or profit in the short term; therefore, the decision to do nothing is most likely to prevail. On the outside of the organisation it might appear that nothing is happening, while on the inside there is a great deal of energy and time being expended on the debate.

Challengers who can cause instability and uncertainty at the right time will cause the Establishment organisation to look frozen on the outside whilst also damaging its spirit on the inside.

In the 1970s Kodak was 75-80% of the market. At the time film sales was almost totally through photo stores. Fuji changed the distribution model. Kodak was impeded to retaliate due to its relationship with the specialist dealers. Their strong relationship stopped them from exploring new distribution channels. There was an avoidance of this difficult change internally. They started to redefine themselves but it was all on paper, nothing changed in the culture. Can this ever be achieved in a strong, dominant player? I tend to hold that if the company has been very strong for a long period of time it is highly unlikely to make this cultural change. (Professor Hermann Simon, ex Board Director, Kodak.)

3.3 Eating Your Young

One of the most important differentiators between Challengers and Establishment organisations is that Challengers are willing to 'eat their young'; they recognise that if they don't someone else will whether they like it or not. If you aren't willing to reinvent what your 'offspring' are, you become stuck. Whether it is killing off one of your own products, divesting part of the group or investing in an emergent product or market it provides a source of energy and renewal. It affects the way that you hire, lead and operate and differentiates organisations that stay on top of the wave rather than those that have to jump from one declining wave on to another. (Clent Richardson, ex VP Worldwide Developer Relations & Solutions Marketing, Apple Inc.)

Whether you are a new entrant to a market or an organisation already established in it, breaking with the immediate past is a key contribution to Purposeful Instability. Challengers don't accept the boundaries of their market as they have been drawn by their own and the market leaders' past successes. Challenger organisations deliberately break with their own immediate past and intentionally reinvent key aspects of the way they work in order to force a rapid reappraisal from their own organisation and the rest of the sector.

Daniel Vasella, the CEO of fourth in market pharmaceutical company Novartis has encouraged his organisation's R&D effort to break with its immediate past to good effect. Most pharmaceutical research is directed towards areas of unmet need that hold huge potential returns in financial terms. These areas of research are also particularly challenging and lead to high rates of failure at later stages when the medicines are tested in humans. This has led to a repeating pattern of high investment for low return in recent years of pharmaceutical research. In 2002 Vasella took a calculated risk and turned his back on this established practice from the past. He chose to back those medicines through to testing in humans only if they were backed by already proven science irrespective of the size of market in financial terms.

Once a medicine had proved its worth against one disease, no matter how small its potential market, then it could be tested against others. One of the most successful recent creations from Novartis is Gleevec. At first it was only approved for a rare blood cancer. Since then it has been shown to be effective against six other life-threatening diseases.[3]

Importantly, in breaking with the immediate past Challenger leaders don't appear to make the past 'wrong'. They find ways of honouring the past without allowing the organisation to stay stuck in it. This makes perfect sense from a psychological perspective because there is less energy wasted by those who were part of creating the past, in proving that the past was 'right'. Instead the energy can be devoted to the present and the future. Challenger leaders who take over organisations in difficulty seem to do this intuitively and naturally.

3.4 Happy People Fighting

> *I asked them about the work hours here when I joined. They said 'we stop work at 17:30 but you don't go home until 20:30. There are three hours of argument and debate at the end of the day. Renzo wants the creative tension that this generates'. (Bob Bayman, Shopping Experience Director, Diesel Jeans.)*

Successful leaders of Challenger Organisations have found a way of working with and practicing the concept of confronting conversations – Happy People Fighting[4] – to the point where it becomes second nature. The benefits of this replicable skill are that it makes leadership more authentic, real and enjoyable; it takes a lot of stress and unresolved tension out of an organisation's culture and strengthens the relationships of those who are working together. Under particularly stressful conditions, familiarity with this work allows projects to keep moving at pace despite the inevitable surprises and difficulties along the way.

This relatable distinction helps people to see the differences between *confronting* (facing into) a performance issue with someone, versus *pussyfooting* around it or *hammering* home the point.[5]

> *The most fundamental thing that has shifted is the size of the relationships in the region. What we have found is that the bigger the relationship, the more that is possible. This is based on how authentic, direct and full are the conversations that take place between individuals and amongst teams. That willingness to go anywhere, we have*

a shared commitment on my Executive Team, to 'nothing unsaid'. Nothing incomplete. This is what leads to the deepest levels of relationship. If any of us pick up through a tone or comment or body language that there is something incomplete between ourselves or other people then we call it out. (Stuart Fletcher, President of International, Diageo.)

Figure 3.2 The Confronting Model.

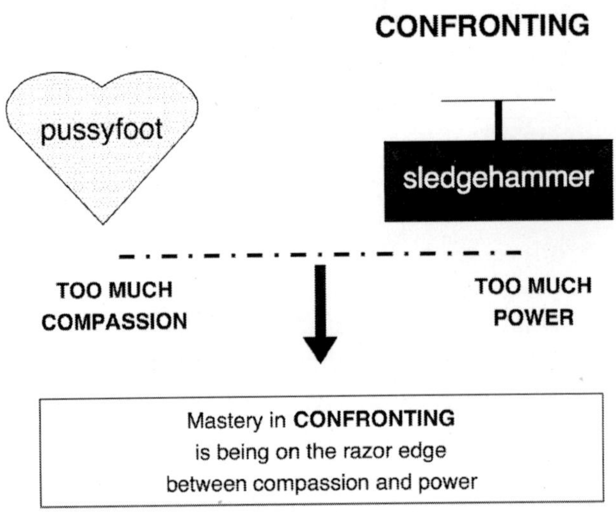

When confronting an issue it can be tempting to slip into a pussyfooting or hammering style which at the time, may seem to be easier than risking hurting someone's feelings or having them disagree with you. The problem of course is that this will usually lead to confusion and the issue is unlikely to be resolved. The pattern then repeats, everything slows down, nothing changes and the issue can become worse. Breaking the pattern and confronting issues in a straight way will result in them being resolved faster and relationships strengthened. Essential requisites for a Challenger Culture.

It strikes me that pussyfooting can contain an over acceptance of the current frame whereas the sledge-hammer wants to destroy it without necessarily having an alternative. I find confronting to be the point of balance in which I can hold the usefulness of the old frame and the contrary signals. It is therefore the best place to witness, facilitate or be the new frame that you want to create. (Clive Bolton, Managing Director, Aviva Equity Release.)

3.5 The Encouraging No

The word 'no' is the most enjoyable word I ever hear because I can say 'why not?' In most organisations if your boss says 'no' then you comply but in a Challenger the word 'no' is a request for more information. Almost every week I used to sit down with the engineers to ask 'why not? (Chris Moss, ex CMO, Virgin Atlantic.)

In a Challenger the word 'no' is a signpost to the possibility of buried treasure rather than a stop sign. It indicates something in the organisation or perhaps even something in the industry sector which has been treated as forbidden territory; a preconception which can be challenged to create a fresh opportunity. Many factors - including common wisdom, past attempts, a limited vision, convenience - create boundaries which are guarded with the word 'no'. Challenger cultures persist with understanding whether the 'no' is to be respected or can become a 'yes and…' or a 'what if…?'.

One of the means by which an Establishment organisation is kept stable is by being anchored in the word ‘no’ for many different contexts. The word ‘no’ can be a powerful force for continuity and security - when the ‘no’ wins, the status quo is protected. If this happens too often, the spirit of the organisation is deadened and this in turn creates new opportunities for the Challenger. One of the ways in which an organisation can continue to refresh itself is by encouraging a culture of ‘why not?’ This in turn is deeply connected to the capability within the organisation to escape the clutches of the 4 ‘A’s.

3.6 Symbols of Re-evaluation

The creation of new symbols is one of the ways that leaders ‘wake up’ their own organisations and the market to the Challenger position.[6] This is not about following the customer; it is about the customer navigating by the position the Challenger adopts. It is saying ‘we are here, we are different, and you need to decide whether we are for you’. This tends to jerk the target consumer out of what they expect the world to be like and starts a new intense relationship with them.

> *When recruiting, a lot of Establishment businesses go out and find people who have done that job before who have got all the tests and they have got some history. When I was recruited to Virgin, I had never worked for an airline before, so I had no understanding of what should and shouldn't be done. I also went and recruited from outside the industry. We made lots of mistakes but they weren't the same mistakes that everyone else was making! We started from a different point so that we could challenge the conventions of everything that had gone before. (Chris Moss, ex CMO, Virgin Airlines.)*

The unchallenged myth in an Establishment organisation is that you are safe if you navigate your organisation by the customer and by what has worked in the past. Challengers look through the other end of the pipe. They are keen to make redundant what has worked in the past and are intentionally looking to create a disturbance that customers have to respond to. Rejection from either their organisation or their customers isn't ideal but is far preferable to the indifference that meets a lot of Establishment offerings. You can't be a Challenger if your stakeholders are indifferent to you.

> *It is risky to turn something off and turn something else on. It takes immersion, courage and commitment. It is painful from the board downwards. But it is usually impossible to focus on the new until you give up some revenue and give up some margin from the old. Human nature does not delay gratification, we want it now. Organisations that have met with any kind of success can fall into that trap. So being able to really separate what you want to sacrifice and what you want to commit to is key. (Clent Richardson, ex VP Worldwide Developer Relations & Solutions Marketing, Apple Inc.)*

Every day offers opportunities to make clear through some symbolic act what the Challenger stands for and how it wants to break from the past. How are you resolving your conflicts? What are the values you are demonstrating through your actions? Who are you recruiting? How are you recruiting them? Who are you replacing? What are you encouraging and recognising? How are you resolving the paradoxes that face you? What are you sacrificing? What are you over-committing to? How are you leading in the tough times? Every choice is a moment in which you can create some symbolic value that has impact far beyond the place where the choice is being enacted.

3.7 Going Through it not Around it

The stories we heard in the research had leaders describing how much they enjoyed the embracing of risk, the opportunity to learn, the unequal competition, the intense desire to win and the sheer fun they have along the way.

> *I am dyslexic so I do believe that Challenger Organisations have fitted for me, it makes you think laterally, my brain works in a different way, but there is also a constant pressure on you. I didn't pass any exams, no O levels or A levels. I couldn't get into the education system that all my friends were in as I couldn't pass the common entrance exams. I have had to fight the establishment from a young age. (Chris Moss, ex CMO, Virgin Airlines.)*

It is not that the leaders concerned didn't experience the same levels of stress associated with anxiety that others do. They reported experiencing the same, but critically that they recovered from the anxiety more quickly and were less likely to respond with defensive mindsets or behaviours that limited their Challenger ability. This set a great example for those following them and over time became an ingrained part of their culture.

> *If anything we are a bit too nice. I think one of the reasons I was brought in is because of an edgy, combative side of me. At heart my CEO is*

a maverick but he can also play the corporate game. Belligerent, opinionated, distinct, I love the fight. (Jim Slater, Marketing Director, Costa Coffee.)

Many of the Challenger leaders we have studied have had backgrounds and developmental experiences that put them into situations of high uncertainty, unpredictability and anxiety at a young age. Their early learning served them well when instilling and containing anxiety in their organisational lives.

A source of this uncertainty and anxiety in the Challenger leader's personal development was often the result of having to live in two worlds at once: the world of the commonly accepted norm and the world in which they were on the outside or edge of things, marked out by their difference. They often survived and thrived in these situations by learning how to live in two worlds at the same time, becoming multi-cultural in a way that allowed them to be accepted by the majority at the same time as challenging the dominant culture's norms and habits.

Being a Challenger you inherently value that which is different. I remember on the first day I started at Mars the HR Manager said I'm really glad you joined because you're different - not the 'Mars type'. Maybe that has just become a self-fulfilling prophecy. I think I have leveraged that to create, exaggerate, and provoke difference and in order to destabilise people's preconceptions about the work. When I am worried about a general indifference to everything being OK I think I can spend some time doing a lot of coaching or I can act out a bit. And for me acting out is the route I have chosen because if you do it credibly and congruently, knowing when to dial it up and dial it down, then it is symbolically very powerful. (Alex de Courcy, Sales and Marketing Director, Consumer and Office Division, 3M.)

Challengers know they are going to cause disturbance and anxiety and they know they have to cause it in order to be successful. If they are going to be able to take their organisations into uncharted territory they have to prepare themselves for the voyage, create some big waves of disturbance and expect the storms that are coming their way. Some of the ways in which they do this are outlined in this chapter and the remaining credos.

There is a word of warning before this chapter is completed. It would be easy to read it and imagine many leaders who fit the criteria under the pattern of purposeful instability. In our experience this can be the case with individuals who have a narcissistic tendency, many of whom we find leading organisations. Narcissists are often successful as they are more willing to take risks, have courage, push through massive transformations, can charm and convert people with their rhetoric and will push the boundaries, which, under the right conditions, enables organisations to thrive – in the short term.

The critical quality that distinguishes them from those that have successfully led Challenger organisations in the long term is that of self-awareness, humility and capacity to learn through personal feedback. Without these qualities the danger is that the culture of the organisation becomes more 'cult like' with followers of the leader charmed and bullied into doing what is wanted by an all-powerful leader. This is not the relational model that underpins the Challenger Spirit we are referring to. The critical quality of Challenger as Learner is the subject of a future chapter.

3.8 The Power of Intention

During instability it is contradictory to hold onto a particular outcome because the moment that you do that, you have invested in a view of the way that you would like things to be, rather than the way that they might emerge. The whole point about instability is that it allows for old ways of doing things to be disrupted, which allows the opportunity for new knowledge to come through. However, if you don't hold on to anything then you become rudderless. This is where intention becomes a very powerful force. You can be consistent in your intention and at the same time learn from and adapt to what emerges. This is the focus of our next Challenger pattern – Hope and Ambition.

> *As a CEO in a listed company the revenue engine is where I want to create stability and predictability but the thing I worry about most is the danger of getting stuck with existing revenue streams and not having any innovation, learning and growth. So I set up units to focus on creating the new, they work in a much less certain and predictable way. I then work on the cusp between the local way of doing things and the benefits of group wide knowledge and consistency. My intention is to deliberately allow difference and latitude to be in tension with efficiency and synergy. (Ian Ailles, European CEO, Wyndham Rentals, Wyndham Worldwide.)*

The Practice Ground

Life has impermanence built into it. It is a thought we can easily cope with until it draws closer to those things that we want to keep the same. It causes us a sort of anxiety that we ameliorate through busyness, control, avoidance, defensiveness, aversion, compensation, and attachment. The outer work of a Challenger is underpinned by the inner work that sees one's reaction against impermanence and works to disentangle the defences.

To help leaders really work effectively with this pattern we have to begin by understanding a concept about anxiety that Dan Siegel[7] described as 'the fence of defence'. Instinctively when faced with uncertainty and impermanence an emotional reaction arises in us, almost instantaneously we experience a reaction of anxiety or fear and this initiates a defensive response. This defensive response has the effect of either shutting down the emotional reaction, which caused the anxiety in the first place, or removing our awareness of it, even though it is still present within us. Either way a fence has been erected around our anxiety.

The limbic area of our brain handles these old defensive reactions known as 'flight, flight and freeze'; they are strong, compelling and fast reactions. Without a leadership practice to help you tune into your reactions and see what is going on, the fences not only keep you disassociated from your feelings but can lead you to develop strategies that are either rigid or chaotic.

If you are having trouble associating this with yourself, think about the last time a significant change was forced upon you and those around you. The anxiety induced by that may have caused people to act in any of the following ways.

Rigidity: head down and maintaining business as usual for as long as possible; refusing to negotiate or entertain the possibility of change; agreeing theoretically but maintaining the same behaviour; clinging to small points of detail and refusing to budge; developing routines and habits and sticking to them; obsessing about aspects of the change.

Chaos: inventing increasingly complex narratives to explain what is happening and why; emotional outbursts; cynicism and humour to deflect from the issues; blaming others and being very vocal about it; enrolling others into your view or actions; imploding into periods of stuck-ness and withdrawal.

Successful Challengers know how to work with impermanence and the creation of instability to unfreeze rigidity in an organisation. In doing so they have done enough inner work so that when the stress comes, as it inevitably will, they can override their instinctive limbic reactions and create situations full of emotional regulation. They don't deliver rhetorical speeches and briefings about the inevitability of change; they embody what it is to live a vital life between the more conventional domains of chaos and rigidity.

In our brains the prefrontal cortex handles issues associated with uncertainty, impermanence and mortality. An indication of what might be happening in the brains of Challengers is provided by the research into those who practice mindfulness, or what we also described in the last chapter as meta-awareness. The fibres in this area of their brain are thicker[8]. In other words these people have increased the physical integration of the areas of their brain where they cope with uncertainty and change; and in doing so they develop an increased ability to regulate their mood, their emotional equilibrium and their resilience. As this part of the brain is also connected to resonance circuits, the research suggests that as we tune into ourselves, our capacity to tune into others increases at the same time. Tuning inwards does enable you to tune outwards with more effectiveness.[9]

With practice, Challengers can begin to orchestrate a complex set of leadership activities: they can cause a shift in stability, they can manage their own reactions to this, they can be alert and sensitive to the reactions and defences of others and they can contain anxiety as it arises in their system.

The Challenger leaders in this book have not chosen to avoid the difficult, waiting until all their needs for certainty are satisfied before they act; or chosen to withdraw their talent from an organisation in a fit of pessimism. They have come to the realisation that in the face of witnessing their organisation as it really is, they must accelerate impermanence, they must intentionally cause instability and they must do it now.

There is a Buddhist question that we use in our work quite frequently: "If only death is certain, but the manner and time of your death is uncertain, what should you do now?"

Getting Stuck In

Inner Work

- How do you tranquilize yourself within your organisation?
- How do you react to impermanence, instability, and ambiguity?
- What is going to take most personal courage?
- How do you role model purposeful instability?
- How do you increase curiosity?

Outer Work

- What do you already know you would not be allowed to do?
- What would be the most symbolic things you could change to indicate you are a serious Challenger?
- How can you move your team out of its comfort zone?
- What purposeful instability can you create to unfreeze your results?
- What is the 'Encouraging No' that you currently face?

Your Notes, Insights and Scribbles

What Good Looks Like

Willing to destabilise themselves and the organisation.

- Willing to break with the past.
- Willing to move away from what they and the team / organisation are good at.
- Challenges the 'sacred cows' in the team and organisation.
- Looks beyond the tried and tested.
- Constantly asks 'why not'.
- Is concerned with what's possible, not what is.
- Tackles fundamental problems head on and doesn't go around them. Is always prepared to create and face difficult circumstances.

Allows possibilities to emerge.

- Creates an environment where anything and everything is up for grabs.
- Talks about 'what ifs' and not 'yes buts'.
- Is clear on what they are trying to cause in the team and organisation.
- Observes and senses what is happening and trusts instinct.
- Steers away from control and compliance towards experimentation and possibility.
- Is able to balance risk against recklessness.
- Knows what to tackle and what to leave alone.

Acts with courage and confidence.

- Shows courage and bravery.
- Is bold and direct.
- Is straight forward.
- Displays an inner confidence.
- Has the courage and confidence to act with conviction.
- Doesn't ask permission.

Is purposeful and commits to action.

- Commits to action even in ambiguity and without all the answers.
- Has the confidence to act before knowing exactly how to achieve things.
- Publically / overtly shows commitment to goals.
- Creates energy for change in the team / organisation.
- Can navigate a path that builds momentum in the team/organisation.
- Can commit in the face of perceived failures.

Self and organisational awareness.

- Constantly seeks to understand how individuals are feeling.
- Seeks to examine how the organisation is changing along the way.
- Understands how things have changed by creating instability.

- Has a questioning mindset that seeks to understand the root cause of issues.
- Continually seeks to understand and reassess the fundamental issues.
- Asks why before what.

HOPE
STREET
SWII

4 Hope and Ambition

Passionate Personal Meaning

This is about knowing what you want to cause, giving the instability you create a purpose. It is about your team, function and organisation being a place you want to be part of. It is investing time in yourselves to create your ambition; sharing this passion and connecting with others, helping them find personal meaning in the work. It is enrolling support not through control, but through context, connection, and conversation. It is about standing up and saying you are the best at something; something you want to make a stand for, something that your staff and your customers can fall in love with and hold you accountable for.

With the instability that Challengers thrive on comes energy, anxiety and difficulty. If there are no containing structures in place organisationally, this disturbance can feel chaotic. Successful Challengers find a way of anchoring their instability in a dream, source of meaning or cause that provides a degree of confidence, hope, ambition, motivation and connection. Vaclav Havel the Czech playwright and politician says that "hope is a feeling that life and work have meaning regardless of the state of the world around you". Hope is the deep substrate that causes ambition to be authentic and compelling. It is the ground from which ambition arises. It is not just about the ra ra of optimism, but a much deeper mindset that calls us to what is right even if the outcome is uncertain. When leaders in Establishment organisations lose hope they either become part of it, or they can no longer bear to stay and seek to withdraw themselves as fast as they can. When we meet a cynical leader in an organistion we know we are facing someone who has lost hope and cannot bear to admit it. We also know that the quality of their ambition is inevitably weakened by their loss of hope. Challenger leaders really do have hope and this is exercised through their ambition. Without it the instability needed by a Challenger could be experienced as unnecessary and generate more stress in the business than it needs or can cope with.

> *Yes we want to be thought leaders, yes we want to create momentum but I think for some of us it is underpinned by another requirement. There is a kind of engrained responsibility that this company should play its part. There are big problems so we have to play a part in the response to those. I think there is, in Challenger organisations, there is a breadth of thinking that doesn't just say we are a business and the financial return is the ultimate*

end point. What I think you see in a Challenger organisation at its core are people that think beyond that financial return and think more broadly.

Of course we will deliver a return every quarter, but beyond that. What are we here to do? Why are we on this planet and how does me working in this company make a difference? Those are pretty bold questions but I wouldn't feel inhibited asking them of anyone here. (Phil Thomson, SVP Global Communications, GlaxoSmithKline.)

4.1 A Place you Want to be Part of

The words are not always the most significant bit. It is the meaning the leaders find (or don't find) behind the words that makes the difference. Finding a way to connect to something in the words that is relevant to us as individuals and as a group. Have we found a place that we want to be part of? That is what is most important. (Mark Martin, HR Director, RBS Insurance.)

Ambition is at the heart of the mindset of a Challenger. The definition articulated in earlier chapters distinguished Challengers as having an 'ambition beyond the resources available to them'. Thinking of their enterprise as an adventure often drives Challengers into the unknown; they love the new, the different, the innovative and the challenging. Their ambition tends to attract people who can personally identify with the standards, care, boldness, courage or integrity expressed in them. If the ambition is at odds with the received wisdom in the sector then all the better; if it challenges the way that dominant competitors or long in the tooth stakeholders want us to see the world then better still. When talking to Challenger leaders about their ambition you can't help but feel a sense of connection to their story, you find yourself willing them to succeed, you notice yourself smiling.

As human beings we are all drawn to metaphors, stories, meaning and a cause that we can put our hearts into. And yet Establishment organisations often revert to meaningless statements as the source of meaning for their organisations. The more machinelike the organisation becomes the less emphasis it puts on the purpose behind the work. A cause to stand for is often undervalued or paid lip service to.

The ambition within Challenger organisations is not the kind found in corporate statements that espouse 'putting the customer first' or 'being number one in…' or 'maximising shareholder value'. These Establishment statements are more driven by a corporate obsession than a dream. Most 'vision' statements from Establishment organisations describe no obvious benefit for the customer. Few of them generate any excitement or inspiration and most leave the reader feeling cold or disconnected.

Those causes that work best in Challenger organisations are simple in their language and structure: short, human, real and able to provide guidance both for the internal culture and the desired customer experience. The purpose becomes embedded in everything the organisation does and is understood by all employees as a guide to making choices and taking action. The question 'why?' is a critical one to spend sufficient time on as a Challenger individual, team, function or business.

> *"Celebrating life everyday everywhere". This purpose was already present at a group level but we worked with it in a way that imbued it with*

more personal meaning for us. In my team we were talking about higher purpose, what was it really all about for the business, in doing that people started to declare what it was about for them personally. When we were searching for a phrase that worked for all of us at an individual and business level, eleven people that had different motivations, expressions, agendas, we realised we had this thing sitting there that summed up what we wanted but we had to relate to it differently, imbue it with a bigger meaning than we had previously seen in it.

We now actively ask people to find and create a deep connection with the Diageo purpose, what are you about in life and how does it fit? When there is that alignment it is very visible and you can see the connection through to improved performance. (Stuart Fletcher, President of International, Diageo.)

A Challenger ambition is visible, simple, consistent and repeated. Importantly, the execution of the cause rather than the words used creates the difference for employees and customers. A great cause can guide what gets done day to day and force big strategic choices in the business. It should define the customer experience and be the benchmark against which the experience is then assessed. At its best it incorporates beliefs about what an organisation stands for and what it stands against. These beliefs are what create engagement and connection in the organisation and with customers.

The cause at the heart of ING Direct is to lead consumers back to savings. In less than a decade the Internet based bank has signed up nearly 8 million customers and generated significant annual profits whilst employing only 2500 people. Whilst the technology and business model in use is impressive what drives the organisation's spirit is the ambition at its heart – to lead consumers back to savings. The company believes it is there to challenge a financial sector that is too interested in encouraging people to borrow and spend which results in saving too little. All the choices made by the organisation are consistent with the ambition and often run against the way the established players in the sector operate.

What you are trying to cause doesn't have to be world changing in a grand sense. You can bring a passion about what you want to challenge, change and effect in your particular realm: to coffee and technology, to vacuum cleaners and pharmaceuticals, to cosmetics and ice cream, to sandwiches and banking. If you are committed to challenging the convention and bringing some originality, momentum and surprise to your market then your organisation and your customers will respond.[1]

4.2 Ambition is not a Dirty Word

Possibility and ambition is not the same as opportunity. You can't define possibility on a spreadsheet you have to talk about it until you get past all the reasonable reasons that get in your way of doing something remarkable. You have to say 'I believe' more than you say 'I think'. (Gordon Ballantyne, Group Managing Director, Telstra.)

In Challenger organisations the question 'why?' is rarely answered through market research with customers and asking them what they want. It more often happens through sitting around, talking and then talking some more about your ambition and desire to make a difference. Tapping into the meaning and possibility that motivates you and your team to get up and get through the difficult times ahead.

> *We know from our research and experience that Challenger organisations, their leaders and teams, need to have ambition beyond their resources, but what of that word "ambition"? What does it mean to have a collective ambition as a leadership team? Where does personal ambition fit, does it add anything of value when leaders and teams are asking themselves the more conventional questions around "what is our vision, mission or purpose?"*
>
> *I think ambition may have been regarded by some as something of a dirty word. The dictionary definition provides some clues as to why, in that it defines ambition as "a strong desire for status wealth or power; a desire to achieve a particular end". This implies some single-minded, gritty, even selfish determination to achieve, but we know that to be successful as a Challenger organisation, or team, you have to be able to harness our collective desires, spirit and energy at all levels of the organisation.*
>
> *Breaking out of our habitual conversations about vision, and into the less common space of conversation about ambition, both collective and personal, can be discomforting and enlightening, confronting and invigorating.*
>
> *Interestingly the word ambition appears next to the word ambivalence in the dictionary. The very*

antithesis of what it takes to challenge yourselves and ultimately your competitors in the market.

In experimenting with this concept with leadership teams in a range of industry sectors I believe there is something of value in inquiring into ambition. All of those teams already had a purpose and/or a vision statement, but in asking them individually to describe their ambition for their part of the organisation something new emerged each time – unvocalised passions and frustrations, profound statements of connection and meaning, levels of doubt and confusion; differences in the size and scope of those ambitions – some big, bold and expansive, others narrower, protected, comfortable – and the realisation that these weren't really ambitions at all but merely flirting with the edge of the status quo. Difficult questions were asked more directly than before and at the same time more compassion and interest was shown in the struggles or aspirations of individual team members. What was clear in the majority of cases was that it isn't sufficient for the team or the organisation to have purpose. Individuals have to truly connect with that purpose and make meaning from it themselves by connecting with their own ambitions.

So what does it take to understand and utilise this collective ambition? We suggest a combination of inner and outer work. The outer work being the quality conversations that uncover the nature of the ambition, that disrupt current habitual thinking and old patterns, that build trust and relationship and a renewed energy and commitment to the future. The inner work being for each individual to come into deeper relationship with their own particular "establishment" thinking and behav-

iour, whether through compassionate confronting by their colleagues or in their own reflections; and develop real clarity on the meaning they are making of their work, what they really believe in as a cause, and therefore their role as leader and team member in seeing that through. (Clare Southall, Relume.)

4.3 Ambition is Uncovered not Manufactured

The writer Joseph Jaworski[2] said, "In a sense real visions are uncovered, not manufactured". This expresses perfectly what the Challengers in our research were saying to us about the way they developed their personal and organisational ambitions.

"In head-to-head taste tests, 7 out of 10 coffee lovers preferred Costa cappuccino to Starbucks". This was a big breakthrough for the business. It really made thousands and thousands of baristas across the business more proud of working for Costa and you could almost feel their chests puffing up with pride, they were now more confident to shout about it.

The advertising campaign picked up on great parts of the business that had always existed. There had always been great coffee, always been hand made by baristi, always had that pride in the business it is just that we started amplifying it and talking about it much more. A hugely successful product built on the back of wanting to be the best and challenge our 10,000 baristas. (Jim Slater, Marketing Director, Costa Coffee.)

What Challengers discover is that they can let go of some of the Establishment ways of developing a sense of the future. The Establishment pattern is usually one based on doing lots of analysis, developing some kind of Utopian view of the future, associating it with targets and then living through repetitive disappointment as the view and targets have to be repetitively adjusted downwards. Developing a view of the future as a formulaic planning or strategy process creates disbelief and collusion rather than energy and commitment.

The Challenger approach loosens the hold of this habitual pattern and trusts more to the emergence of 'bottom up' insights. The leaders involved develop a better capacity for sensing and accessing the depth of their current experience.

> *Curiosity is not something that you can coach easily, but it is at the root of almost anything good that happens in business. The best example of that here - if you are an Account Manager in the FMCG sector - take ten of them, half of them won't spend enough time in customer stores. Of the half that do go out to stores most will visit their part of the store to confirm their biases. But the very best don't go to confirm what they know until they have done the rest of the store and had a look at what is happening elsewhere. The benefit of this way of approaching things is to continuously understand what is possible. Very often we are told by our customers and our colleagues what is possible to achieve and we don't validate that in any way. I am always saying to my team let's go and have a look elsewhere and tune in to what is going on. At the root of any ambition is the question 'I wonder why?'. Everything comes back to curiosity for me.*

(Alex de Courcy, Sales and Marketing Director, Consumer and Office Division, 3M.)

A good starting point for tuning in to the Challenger organisation is usually looking for what is the best of the present. Being clear and confident about the bright spots of your current business can be very persuasive. It's not a communication exercise without any foundation in reality; it is consistent with the way your organisation behaves today.

'The Power of Dreams'. What does that mean exactly? Or even roughly? It sounds like a cheesy self-help book by 'Doctor' Marybeth P. Scrimshanker. Or worse - one of those empty global corporation slogans. In fact, this was a global corporation slogan - for Honda - and the UK marketing team's first instinct was to hope that if they ignored it for long enough, it might go away.

It was never going to go away, and that turned out to be a good thing. Although The Power of Dreams was a global corporation slogan, it certainly wasn't an empty one. In rummaging for insights that might bring about a revaluation of Honda, a crucial breakthrough was made by Wieden and Kennedy, Honda's advertising agency. At first you couldn't see it for looking. The breakthrough came with the realisation that something internal could be used as the external solution. The Power of Dreams was true to the spirit of how the corporation thought and acted. And how.

The values of the company's creator were still coursing through the veins of its culture. Soichiro Honda was relentlessly passionate about engines, optimistically imaginative, socially responsible… and just a little bit bonkers. In a nice way. He bequeathed such attributes to the company in a legacy that still walks the Honda corridors today. It had been under their noses the whole time, but marketing had never before thought to fashion this into a weapon for brand communications.

A full appreciation of the potency of Honda's DNA turned to frustration that it wasn't understood outside. And so the marketing strategy was born; to expose the inner truth about Honda. No global focus groups scavenging for consumer insights along with the other car manufacturers. No marketing away days to retrofit a brand vision to customer needs. Instead, the confidence to believe that telling people the truth about 'Hondaness' would do the job. The job being to make them revalue the brand and feel better about owning one. In other words, to make them want a Honda. Actually, not in other words… those are the exact words. (Wieden and Kennedy, Submission for Marketing Society Awards 2004).[3]

Something else about ambition that sets Challengers apart from the Establishment is that they often can't compete on all fronts at the same time. This helps with ambition as they often become known for making the running in their sector on some parameter. Being the best at something is at the heart of many Challenger ambitions and success stories.

We were a sleeping giant with a number two mindset. We lacked self-confidence, we believed our competitors were better than we were and it coloured everything we did. We had to stand up and say we were the best at something. One way we tackled this was to re-launch Holiday Inn. A total brand refresh, taking out 1200 underperforming hotels, adding around 1800 newly built ones, refreshing the remainder and completely reworking the guest experience with our staff. We did this in just over two years. (Richard Solomons, CEO, Intercontinental Hotel Group.)

In the stories we heard about successful Challenger ambitions coming to life, there was always an associated energy put into lots and lots of conversations. We rush past meaning, context and possibility too quickly in the conversations we have in Establishment organisations. This is in contrast to the amount of time and energy that is expended on corporate obsessions, defining competencies so that everyone know what a role looks like, providing skills training so that everyone has the tools to do a good job, putting in place processes and measures so that all of this can be tracked – constantly. But providing people with some ambition, hope and belief, with a real reason for doing what they are doing is something that is over indexed against in a Challenger organisation.

Creating a dream is one thing but getting people to believe it is possible is very different. It requires a big focus on conversations, stories, and symbols - relationship processes that are created for the purpose. Belief is multi dimensional: believing in yourself that you have the skills, capabilities to undertake the challenge; belief in the people around you not to criticise or attack when things don't go right; belief that you can make a difference; belief in the organisation's appetite to give you the space and the remit to act.

For me it starts with my own belief: can I quell the butterflies in my stomach; can I really see in my mind the final destination; can I stay true to the ambition and therefore authentic; will I waver when the going gets tough? (Russell Taylor, VP Business Development and On Line. Everything Everywhere.)

4.4 Customers Falling in Love

The greatest ambitions, dreams and causes create an emotional experience for your customers that equates to falling in love. We believe great Challenger organisations are built on great customer experiences that spark interest and ultimately mean that loyalty is impenetrable and advocacy is wide ranging.

What you get when you are in love is magic - magic moments of contact, humour, feeling, uniqueness and trust. Who wouldn't want to be part of an organisation that makes you feel like that, and if you were part of one, who wouldn't want to talk about it? People in love are obsessed by their passion and they want to talk about their partners all the time! Frankly, it is hard to shut them up. They do it because by talking about the person, they are bringing the experience to life for themselves all over again. We believe this is also what happens when employees and customers fall in love with a Challenger brand and organisation. There is a sense of curiosity or adventure or excitement or delight or inspiration in the relationship; sometimes all of these qualities combined!

The opposite of falling in love can be feeling fear. Causing their employees to be fearful is something that is encountered all too often in Establishment organisations. This internal fear drips through to their customers in all kinds of visible and invisible ways. The environments seem surrounded by messages of fear, concern, guilt and unhelpful anxiety.

Frightened people can't be themselves. Frightened people can't be inspiring. Frightened people behind brands can't create inspiring brand experiences. Fear in organisational life kills learning and exploration. It stops people stepping out beyond the boundaries of what they thought possible. It stops people expressing themselves.

4.5 Internal Experience Drives External Experience

Ultimately the effectiveness of your ambition can only be measured by the way your customers experience you when they touch the Challenger organisation. We are always curious about the experience we receive when we are a customer of an organisation or brand and have looked hard for connections between the internal Challenger or Establishment spirit and the external manifestation of that spirit.

A recent experience with Prêt a Manger gave us a number of sources of inspiration, seeing in practice some of the principles we hold dear. This was a Challenger spirit in operation.

> *Everything is driven by our belief in the quality of our food. Good tasting, natural, preservative free and we always make it on site. Currently we have 26 freshly made items on display on any one day.*

I hate going to a city and not being able to find anything healthy and cheap to eat. We like good food and serving customers well. To qualify to become a sandwich maker in our business takes a year. We take it very seriously. (Julian Metcalfe, Co-Founder and CEO, Prêt a Manger.)

Simple examples of the Challenger Spirit being lived day to day that we won't forget include:

- That it was so easy to go and hang out with them for a day. Only one telephone call to a customer service agent who didn't need to check with anyone at 'head office' if it was okay for us to visit. Just asked us which store we would prefer and set the date up.

- That there really was a kitchen making fresh food inside every establishment. We always imagined the 'fresh' food was prepared somewhere else and shipped in.

- That there was a continuous focus on learning. It was done with a sense of joy and shared publicly rather than hidden away somewhere. After our morning shift making sandwiches and salads was over one of the products was randomly selected from the shop front and brought back to the kitchen. The person responsible for making it stripped the sandwich down in front of her colleagues looking for feedback and learning on presentation, contents and preparation. There was no fear in this act, no manager was looking over her shoulder, this was an act of responsibility and learning.

- That the smiles in the kitchen were genuinely replicated for the customers in front of house. Relationships mattered in this culture and this was being transmitted to the customers in brief, high impact interactions.

- That the staff preparing sandwiches were able to drop everything and serve a customer if it was likely that someone was going to be waiting more than a minute to be served. For people who were partly assessed on the speed of their manufacturing, this choice to serve rather than make the sandwich numbers look good was pervasive and real.

This shop had no reason to try and look good in front of us. We were a couple of men from an office on the same road as them, interested in learning about what they do and how they do it. The organisation has put into practice their beliefs on getting the internal service quality right and they are rewarded on a number of metrics. Not least that they are rewarded well for their efforts at retaining and developing their people. Currently, 75% of Prêt Managers began their careers as Team Members.

4.6 A Cause is for Life, not Just for Christmas

Ryanair refusing to comply with European legislation on compensation of stranded travellers. Google professing that it was possible to make money without doing evil then compromising their values so that they could access the market in China. Believing that Apple thinks differently and then having them deny obvious hardware and software failings with the iPhone 4. Prêt a Manger selling a stake to McDonalds, Bodyshop to L'Oreal, Innocent to Coca Cola, Green and Blacks to Cadburys - selling all or part of their Challenger business to Establishment organisations that they had appeared to stand 'against'.

A Challenger ambition is regularly tested through the choices that are made every day in the business. Are the choices being made consistent with the ambition and values that you are building your business around? In the unstable environments that Challengers thrive in navigating these choices takes on a different form to that inside Establishment organisations. The Establishment environment is more mechanised, stable and with less pace so choices are more often guided by processes, controls, rules and large manuals. The Challenger environment has more instability, pace and disturbance built into it so has to be more informed by the cause and values the Challenger espouses.

It is all too easy in the heat of day-to-day challenges to end up compromising yourself and your ambition. To be awake to this state is a significant test. Especially when you are at the point of everything being familiar and heading towards success. At the point you are tested – will you trade everything you have committed to for ease, pragmatism or apathy? Will you erode your integrity slice by slice until it is all gone? Will you step over a predicament, pretend not to notice, hoping that someone else will pick it up or that it will go unnoticed?

> *The people working in the food industry are treated pretty poorly and not looked up to in the UK and US cultures. When we started, these young people had little hope, they weren't trusted and they weren't treated well. I started concentrating on what was wrong here, what do I have to do to change this? The closer I got to the staff in the first few shops the more I realised we had a massive problem. (Julian Metcalfe, Co-Founder and CEO, Prêt a Manger.)*

In a Challenger organisation these difficulties are all opportunities against which to test and further develop your ambition. If approached in the right way, the ambition becomes more visible and detailed to you through its exposure to the changing reality of the business you are in. This is all part of the process of discovering rather than manufacturing your ambition.[4]

If a Challenger organisation has delivered a customer experience that has caused its customers to fall in love with the offering, then the disappointment if they feel let down is similarly extreme. Remember they are buying hope and ambition as well as a product or service. We have all experienced the kind of shock that feels like a promise we believed was being broken. We have invested our emotion into an organisation and don't like how it feels.

The Practice Ground

In a coaching conversation with a bright and talented Challenger leader, we uncovered a moment, when he was doing some reflection on his leadership purpose. As he was writing, a phrase literally popped out on the page. He had written, "to give people hope". He turned red, shifted on his seat and then laughed uncomfortably about it before trying to rub it out. When we slowed the whole experience down and asked him to work more on his inner reactions, this is what he said: "well actually I do really believe that, it is important to me that I help my people feel real hope about the future of this organisation and about the value of the contribution they are making. But I could never say it out loud, it just feels too emotional!"

The Establishment within us often likes to dampen down any sentiment or energetic response that feels outside the boundary of what is conventionally acceptable. We should feel emotional about our hope and ambition for our businesses. We devote much of our lives to our corporate organisations; people from all backgrounds across the world are employed by them or impacted by them.

Senge et al[4] proposed, "Most visions that management teams come up with are superficial. Even if they embody a lot of good thinking; they are still the product of a fragmented awareness, and usually of one or two people's ideas imposed upon the group."

The moment you are faced with developing ambition and creating hope you have to realize that you need to dig much deeper to access what will create a strong 'yes' inside you and others. Mostly these development processes in organisations have been relegated to formulae. The monoculture of Establishment practices, no matter what company you work for, means that a top down habitual way of thinking about vision and then a habitual process for generating it dominates.

Add in the absence of leaders really tuning-in to the organisational reality and you have a recipe for aspirations that are an unhappy combination of extending the past; Establishment dressed up in Challenger language; avoidance of any purposeful instability and something so bland that you can hardly say no to it. But could you say a very strong and compelling 'yes'?

Joseph Jaworski[5] said, "In a sense real visions are uncovered, not manufactured". This chimes well with the experience of our leaders who begin to develop meta-awareness. What they discover is that they can loosen the hold of their habitual thinking and trust the emergence of their 'bottom up' insights. They have a better capacity for sensing and they can access more of the depth of their experience. When we use an exercise designed to help people work on their hope and ambition, we notice a marked difference in the quality of responses between groups practicing awareness and those that treat the task as a formula. With the former group we find they are more creative, passionate, and generate breakthroughs. In addition they create ideas that have more heart in them and deeply affect those listening. Without doubt these are leaders you would want to follow.

The Challengers in this book are not ashamed to feel deeply, they are not uncomfortable with caring about hope and expressing it. It is the depth of their dreams and their courage to stand by them that makes them compelling to others. They are not all involved in great social projects, they simply care about their organisational life in all its forms no matter how apparently mundane. They care enough to turn the ordinary into the extraordinary.

Getting Stuck In

Inner Work

- How fully do you allow yourself to dream about success?
- How do you actively inspire yourself?
- What obsesses you at work and dominates your headspace? What gives you energy?
- Where are you dampening your own creativity?
- How would you describe your own Challenger Spirit?

Outer Work

- How often do you talk with your team about possibility?
- How can you develop a conversation with your stakeholders that encourages them to dream?
- What is worth standing for?
- What are you trying to cause?
- What story or image best captures your Challenger dream for your organisation?

Your Notes, Insights and Scribbles

What Good Looks Like

Has personal meaning in their work

- Is clear about who they are and why they are here.
- Unwavering belief in their reason for being.
- Has a deep rooted belief in what they are trying to achieve.

Openly shares their personal meaning and radiates inspiration.

- Everyone knows what they are about and their connection to the work.
- You know what they stand for.
- People know what they are passionate about and why.
- They show a real zeal about their work.
- They do everything wholeheartedly.
- Their passion and enthusiasm is infectious.
- Meaning drives and sustains their energy at work.

What you see is what you get.

- You know what you'll get because they are open and transparent about what is important to them.
- They are predictable because you know what they think.
- People don't need to check back for an opinion; you know what they'll say because you know what they believe.

- They are consistent in thought and action.
- They are disarmingly straightforward.

Creates and connects meaning for others.

- Makes every effort to build relationships and connect with people inside and outside the team.
- Helps create meaning in their work for every individual in the team.
- Uses metaphors and imagery to connect with others.
- Ensures that individual meaning connects to that of the organisation.
- Appeals to people's values, hopes and aspirations.
- Gives people the freedom to be themselves and encourages individuality and diversity.
- Encourages/prioritises meaning in people ahead of controlling and checking work.
- Continually tests how people are directionally aligned.
- Will not rest until meaning is created between people and groups.

Captivating support in the organisation.

- Has an absolute belief that the team/organisation can be the best but is not yet there.
- Effectively communicates and wins support for a new and different agenda.
- Creates a compelling case for the future.
- Influences at all levels in the organisation.

- Effectively finds a path through the politics.
- Turns sceptics into advocates.
- Is able to challenge habitual thinking.
- Is able to navigate through antagonism and accepts conflict as part of the process.
- Insightful about others and how best to influence them.

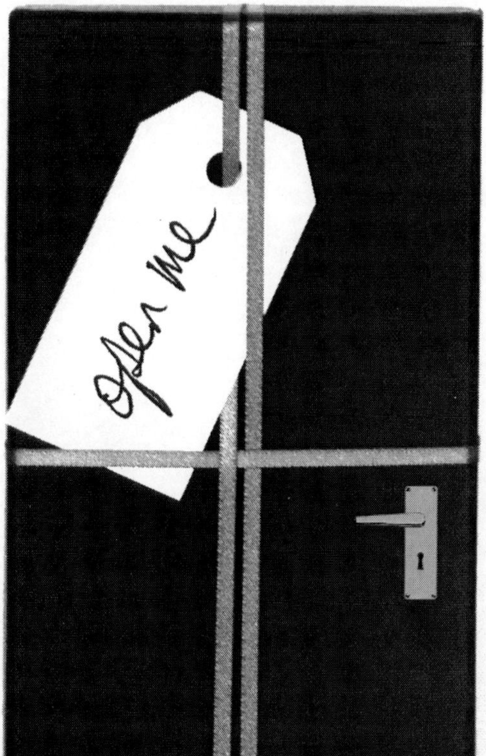
Open me

5 Challenger as Learner

A Begin Again Mind

This is about redefining and welcoming your ignorance. It is about generating momentum through learning at a faster rate than your competitors, establishing yourself as a thought leader. It is seeing every situation as an opportunity to learn and not reaching for what is already known. It is constantly looking for new sources of learning from a wider field beyond your specialism. It is creating a habit of hypothesising, experimenting and adapting. It is seeing and releasing the energy that learning brings. It is infecting others with a desire to learn and deliberately taking people outside their comfort zone to get breakthrough results. It is understanding how and where stress can block learning and being able to use this anxiety to move things into new areas. It is a welcoming of the learning in the twists, turns, difficulties and breakdowns along the way. It is finding a way to do all of this together in an open and public way so that collective learning takes place.

5.1 Momentum over Mass

> *We are the smallest of the top four in terms of retail banking. So we are thinking how can we grow our share when we have ruled out inorganic growth? We want to take a leadership position, that doesn't necessarily mean we will have the most share but that we are thought of as the thought leader in the eyes of our customers.*
>
> *At an all time low for trust in the banks, we are choosing to differentiate ourselves as the leaders in terms of reputation. This will be our thought leadership position reflected in everything we do. (Glenn King, CEO Servco, National Australia Bank.)*

Challengers, much more than Establishment organisations, can never afford to be static. The underlying driver for a Challenger is momentum – the sense that the organisation is making the running in a particular sector. The fuel for this momentum is the ideas and experiments that come from an emphasis on learning. Learning at a faster rate than the Establishment organisation. While a Challenger rarely has the luxury of being a market leader in terms of share it can make progress by establishing itself as a thought leader in the sector. This establishes you in the eyes of your customers, stakeholders and organisation as being the one to keep an eye on as the source of breakthroughs, innovation and new ideas.[1]

Establishment players often get weighed down by their own mass, a mass that can be a function of size but is also impacted by the emphasis on 'making things certain'. This is particularly present at the time of annual/ strategic planning. For Challengers, strategic planning is a learning process. For Establishment organisations it is mostly a process of data collection so that a picture of certainty can be presented to the board and the analysts.

It is not that planning is ignored in a Challenger organisation but that the emphasis is more on uncertainty than it is on certainty. Uncertainty is what a Challenger thrives on so pushing oneself into the learning zone, reflecting and acting quickly is more important than being absolutely 'sure' about a forecast, plan or set of numbers.

> *One of the things we've historically done well is not to become too obsessed with 3-year planning as a management tool. A small team manages the 3-year planning process internally, on behalf of the CEO. Naturally the 3-year plan is vitally important in agreeing top-down financial targets with our shareholder. But the actual plan that we execute to meet these targets is built in a different way. It is built bottom-up by the business on-the-ground. By contrast in some other businesses I've worked in, the 3-year plan is treated as a detailed blueprint for running all areas of the business top-to-bottom – a bit like the old Soviet planning system during the Cold War. In times of unprecedented change having an operational plan that's grounded in the market and which is agile and flexible is vitally important. (Robert Franks, Senior Strategist, Telefonica O2 UK.)*

The Challenger teams pursued strategic conversation in a way that focussed on taking action, gathering data on the effect quickly, incorporating learning and rapid adjustment. They were not afraid to kill a strategic direction if they found it to be flawed and they did this quickly.

The first half of this chapter considers the inner work that may be necessary in order that you can lead with momentum. The desired thought leadership is often imagined as knowing more, better or faster than your competitors but in order to achieve this you first have to connect with what you don't know, your ignorance, to sit on the edge of your learning zone rather than inside your comfort zone; to develop an understanding of the environmental conditions under which you particularly prosper and of those that leave you feeling limited or constrained. To be aware of the ways in which you might sabotage yourself, seeing the familiar patterns of being that limit your potential to view your leadership, team, function, organisation or sector with new eyes.

The second half of the chapter outlines some ways in which the outer work of Challenger as Learner manifests in the organisations we have researched, working with experimentation, making breakthroughs out of breakdowns and observing the processes by which Challengers learn collectively as well as individually.

> *When I was with Twinings we were constantly going after PG Tips. What we did and what it felt like was a kind of restless dissatisfaction. Every day we wanted to make up some ground in some way on the market leader. (Alex de Courcy, Sales and Marketing Director, Consumer and Office Division,3M.)*

5.2 Working with our Ignorance

There is a tendency in Establishment organisations to think that we are paid for what we know and that our historic experience is very useful to us. Of course that is true, where would we be without our experiences? The problem this generates for Challengers is that when theyare responsible for destabilising the status quo, prior experience can become a straight jacket. If we are not truly awake we end up resting on past experiences and simply making our current situations fit what has gone before.

Very few people who are successful leaders in organisations have small egos. Knowledge and experience strengthen our ego and help with our resilience in difficult times. A strong ego can also become a prison – to the point where genuine discovery, creativity and exploration are reduced without us even noticing it. The first sign of this may be when we notice our energy is diminishing, or we find an increase in our boredom levels. If we are aware enough we can take the hint and begin to accept we must stop hiding behind what we know and come into a more open acceptance of what we don't know.

We have chosen the word *ignorance* as a strong provocation. Ignorance gets a bit of a bad press doesn't it? We tend to think of it as a negative quality, one to be avoided. When we describe someone as ignorant we are generally being judgmental and critical.

However, in this context, we want to elevate the state of ignorance to an attitude of mind that is not limited by ego, competition, grasping onto status, fear of not knowing, or a desire to look good. In the way *we* understand ignorance, it is a deep willingness to rest in questions that we do not know the answer to, and to be willing to stay there a little longer than our own comfort would normally allow, for the sake of making a breakthrough.

Underpinning this work is a gradual but profound acceptance that leaders can also be rewarded for facing into what is unknown and encouraging their teams to do the same.

As Challenger organisations warm up to the idea that ignorance is okay, they find more energy for tackling issues that at first seem insurmountable. They relish the energy and creativity it takes to find a path to a breakthrough, rather than shoe horning an old solution in a rehashed way.

What we are calling for is a shift in our relationship to what we do not know, so that we can embrace ignorance as a powerful starting point for making significant breakthroughs. It begins with our own attitudes to ignorance. It begins with seeing ourselves as open to inquiry, to newness and to having faith that by facing into the unknown we can find solutions that are fresh and satisfying.

What does it mean to not know in business when most of us feel paid to have an opinion that we can reach for quickly? In practice, it means not reaching for our habitual assumptions, our quick fixes and our already thought through solutions. It means taking a purposeful pause before we get into judgement, to give curiosity a chance to breathe. It means being open to the fact that you may not know; you may just think you do.

5.3 The Outer Reaches of your Learning Zone

In a Challenger, leadership is required that protects space for learning and experimentation, (we call this the learning zone); resisting the pull exerted by the existing pattern to return to old ways of being (we call this the comfort zone).

Figure 5.1 The Learning Zone.

As an organisation starts to experiment with new ways of being, an edge of uncertainty surfaces between the old state and the new one, between the comfort zone and the learning zone. Leading through this time is a critical success factor for the future success of a Challenger culture.

> *As we have studied our breakthroughs we have been interested in how much risk is possible. We have studied this factor as being a key to creativity and unlocking performance in its broadest sense. We learned to appreciate that most risk is about risk to 'me'. How am I going to look, what are people going to say, what are the consequences for my progression, my reputation? It is all about me. We talk about risk to the business but we*

have learned that most risk that stops us doing positive things for the business is the risk to self. When you really look at that, the tolerance level of the business to risk is incredibly high. Most risk is usually an illusion and this is what stops innovation. As we get better at identifying and naming the illusion our innovation and general performance improves. Over the past year 50% of our growth has come from innovation. (Stuart Fletcher, President of International, Diageo.)

When things start to shift in organisations as people try things, experiment and evolve, we can experience this as chaotic uncertainty. We should look at uncertainty and what we have taught ourselves to believe about it as a state.

Conventional Establishment views about the uncertainty caused by being in the Learning Zone:

- Fear and dislike
- Out of control
- Difficult to know what is going on
- Confusing
- Lacking direction or clarity
- Disorder
- The unknown
- Anxiety inducing
- Possibly creative
- Okay as long as it doesn't go on for too long
- Not what we are here for
- Speed through it

- Alarming

But what if the views in a Challenger could be shifted to see it as:

- An indication of something ingrained beginning to melt
- A possibility
- An alchemical experience
- An expression of learning in action
- Signs of movement
- A call for equanimity rather than panic
- A release of energy
- A moment to become curious
- People doing what you have asked them to do
- An early stage in making something real

If we take the conventional view then the traditional leadership response to the learning zone and signs of uncertainty is force, control and a swing away from learning towards constraint: a move away from the learning zone back to the comfort zone. At this point all the energy that was poured into getting people to step out in the first place is suddenly curtailed or strangled; cynicism and cliché arise in the minds of employees.

However the alternative interpretations of uncertainty and learning create a new mindset across a Challenger business and invite a more spacious, measured response to chaotic elements in the system. Leaders with this commitment are working at creating Challenger environments in their businesses. They are staying focused on the organisational shift and not only their own anxieties.

We have moved a long way over the past 2 years. From a parental style of relationship riddled with performance issues and a lack of authenticity to a more honest learning environment, where we regularly confront the brutal truth – in terms of business issues, people issues and wider strategic issues. In dealing with the good, the bad and the ugly we have become more challenging of what we don't know. More challenging of our colleagues and ourselves and this has supported the business in delivering significant outperformance in the markets in which we operate. (Alex de Courcy, Sales and Marketing Director, Consumer and Office Division, 3M.)

If you are going to lead an organisation into its learning zone you are going to be better equipped if you have examined your own comfort zone, learning zone and 'oh hell' zone. When you reflect on what stops you moving from your comfort zone into your learning zone, what do you identify? If you removed one fear from your learning zone what would it be? What are the conditions that allow you to stay in your learning zone and not shrink back? How can you recreate them more consistently? If your Challenger is going to be successful what is the key piece of learning is needed in your own leadership?

5.4 Your Leadership Conditions

A normally very competent leader in a global business was experiencing high stress levels during a complex buy out. His frustration was spilling over into badgering behaviour and anxiety that things were going to go wrong.

After a coaching session he was able to see that he was good at leading when there were clear goals, very close teamwork and he felt trusted. When we looked at the conditions that were in existence at that time, he could see that the goals were diffuse and changing, the team was virtual and fairly newly formed and he had a new boss. In other words the conditions he found most favourable to his leadership were currently absent.

Conditions may be neither good nor bad, but they can have a strong influence on making our leadership effectiveness *conditional*, and for most of the time we don't even realise that is the case. When things are going well and are stable we probably wouldn't give it much consideration. When things are unstable and uncertain, it is more likely that the conditions under which we do well are harder to hold on to.

Some of us find it difficult to accept that we have conditions, mainly because we interpret *conditions* as negative. We think that we should not have them and so we reject the possibility that each of us has some preferences.

Once our leader realised that he needed certain conditions to be effective, he was able to explore in more depth how he could go about creating some of those conditions. He met the executive team, shared what he had learned and helped each of them to work out where they were experiencing stress and feelings of reduced ability. Collectively they found some shared conditions that were missing that they could do something about. They produced a plan to increase their effectiveness. Stress levels went down quickly.

But there is a deeper issue here. We believe that the next level of development, beyond recreating the conditions that we need to be more effective as leaders, is to move to a position where we can truly lead without any of our conditions being available to us: stepping out onto uncertain ground and leading despite the prevalent conditions, not because of them. We believe this is one of the marks of a Challenger Leader.

> *There was a moment in the situation when some of the most compelling conditions that the executive team were attached to revealed themselves to be unalterable. They all wanted a sense of closer involvement in what was happening and to feel they were trusted. These are not unreasonable conditions, but the special circumstances of the buyout meant that they could not be met and sustained. Clinging to them was creating a very powerful sense of injustice and impotence. The effect of this was felt directly by the staff led by this team.*
>
> *There came a painful but paradoxically liberating moment when those leaders in the executive team had to accept that the absence of a condition that was activating them so much was a call to step out and lead without the condition being present – in other words to transcend their needs and lead from nothing. The released energy in each of them was remarkable to witness.*

For this aspiration to take hold in us, we have to begin by discovering and acknowledging what our conditions for leadership are and how they affect us. Only when we have the humility to do this inner work can we begin the journey of transcending the conditions that sometimes trap us. The remainder of this chapter examines some of the ways that Challenger as Learner expresses itself through outer work.

5.5 Less Judging and More Jumping

> *Like many companies, we have classic examples where we thought we knew what we were going to do and had done our research & planning and then seen a project take much longer and cost more than we thought. So now we are learning from watching the internet companies, involving customers much more, working with the principle of co-creation, beta testing things before they are launched. As a result our success rate, time to market and quality all improve. But of course you can't have the illusion of confidence that a perfect plan or spreadsheets give you.(Robert Franks, Senior Strategist, Telefonica O2 UK.)*

The way Challenger strategies get developed is through experimentation. At their heart strategy development processes are about experimental learning. The relative lack of resources or high need for urgency in some Challenger organisations cause them to have to think differently about strategy from those leading an Establishment business. In an Establishment business, strategy is often a product of much analysis, planning, scenarios, spreadsheets, stakeholder engagement and approval committees. In a Challenger business strategy evolves (quickly) through experimentation. What are the assumptions we want to test? What are the hypotheses we need some real experience to validate? Where can we start something small so that we can learn fast and then try again? What is the smallest amount of funding with which we could test our ideas in the real market?

Experiments don't carry the weight of Establishment strategy processes. They have a momentum of their own and as the data are gathered, the insights distilled and the hypotheses validated or challenged, the strategy is formulated and enacted both at the same time.

Over time the stories of success from Challenger organisations become mythologies about a leader's great ability to see trends no one else would have predicted, to define strategies that surprised the market and were the results of much strategic thought, planning and foresight. But the day-to-day reality when we hear the Challenger stories is often very different and much more experimental in its tone.

This experimental philosophy is increasingly enabled by technology and the vast amounts of data that are available to most businesses. In addition to data that can be purchased increasingly cheaply, the advent of web-based communities is providing a novel form of data that provides quick feedback for any experiment that is carried out.

> *I like the fact this is a very transparent non hierarchical company, first names, no bull shit, cut to the chase and get stuff done. I love the bias for action, they want to make things happen and not analyse them to death.The nice thing about the Internet is that it is very easy to experiment and if you get it wrong you just rub it out and start again. The Establishment competitors create a campaign, get it into the shops, formulate catalogues, much more planning goes into those things, I can just try out a pricing strategy and change it instantly if it isn't bringing us the volume/ margin mix or the feedback we want. The technology and structure we*

have encourages us to experiment but it wouldn't be enough without the culture to back it up.(Brian McBride, CEO, Amazon UK.)

We are fast approaching a time when almost every interaction with a customer could be analysed, experimented with and generate insights. Segmentation, pricing, promotion, loyalty, branding, could be researched in an instant. No technology though, however effective, is going to be of use if the Challenger as Learner mindset isn't part of the organisation's culture and spirit.

5.6 Use Breakdowns for Breakthroughs

One of the quickest ways to destroy energy in a Challenger Culture is for leaders and their teams to experiment and for their mistakes to be punished.This creates disenchantment, a sense of violation and a feeling that they have been misled.

Challenger leaders prefer to distinguish mistakes as breakdowns that, if worked with mindfully, can generate big breakthroughs for the next stage of the work that is in difficulty. Challenger cultures are defined by how leaders and teams relate to breakdowns. Are breakdowns experienced as a time when leaders snatch back control or a time when teams generate new breakthroughs together?

Traditional ways of relating to breakdowns are "*I'm right – you're wrong*", needing to look good, blame or rejection, justification, loss of face, making excuses, anger and victim based behaviour. The traditional response comes very much from a place of the leader having 'power over' others.

An alternative approach emphasises a way of dealing with breakdowns that comes from a place of 'power with'. It encourages participants to separate their emotional interpretation of what happened from the mere facts and to stay in relationship whilst the breakdown is being worked through; to identify the genesis of the breakdown in their own leadership rather than in blaming someone a long way down the line; and to make empowered requests of and promises toeach other for the next stage of the work.

Netflix is a Challenger organisation that has successfully challenged the Establishment organisation Blockbuster in the USA DVD Rental market. A recently published document on the Netflix culture reinforces the need to work with breakdowns if you are a Challenger. They describe the need for rapid recovery rather than avoidance of error.

> *We're in a creative-inventive market, not a safety-critical market like medicine or nuclear power. You may have heard preventing error is cheaper than fixing it. Yes, in manufacturing or medicine but not so in creative environments. Mostly, Rapid Recovery is the right model.(Netflix Guide on our Freedom and Responsibility Culture 2009.)*

5.7 Learning Together

> *To keep things on track, we have a thing called the Brain Trust, made up of all our high-level producers, directors and animators. The Brain Trust meetings are crucial, and we all have to check our egos at the door. Nobody will ever pretend things are working if they're clearly not – and all the people having their say are key*

creatives, not detached studio money men." (Lee Unkrich, Director, Pixar.)[2]

It didn't matter what they called the process – 'Huddles' or 'Scrums' or 'Self and Peer Assessment' or 'Action Learning' or 'Post Action Review'. These organisations had teams of people leading them that were adept at regular team conversations focussed on both the immediate actions they were undertaking and the immediate learning that was being generated. This was not a navel gazing exercise; it was real, brutally honest and very applicable.

The teams that were excellent at this way of working were embracing the uncertainty and diversity of opinion that successful Challenger organisations stimulate. The processes were full of high quality, often uncomfortable conversation but the anxiety so created was part of the process and was worked through rather than avoided.

The discipline of maintaining this learning process (some organisations were having short conversations daily) was a key part of long-term success. There were always many reasonable reasons as to why this time could be sacrificed if the team wasn't vigilant about it.

5.8 The Worse We Look, the Better We do

Bruce Herreld led IBM's strategy unit during the period that it recovered from a 'near death' experience in the 1990s. Speaking at the Harvard Business School's Strategy Conference in 2008 he talked about finding out who the 'red team' was for any project i.e. the team inside IBM with the strongest opposing view. When there was an issue that was complex and difficult or where there was a situation where things had not gone as planned he used to convene a meeting involving the people with different views and he would open it with the lines "the worse we look in here, the better we will do out there".

It was a strong invitation, in fact an instruction, for people not to try to look good or to dress up bad news. There was a commitment to exploring, understanding and learning which was instrumental in IBM rediscovering its Challenger spirit.

The Practice Ground

Leading as a Challenger and learning are intimately connected. If you are not learning then you are not leading – you are acting for your salary. Learning in some Establishment organisations has deteriorated to another means by which you can look good rather than be real as a leader. The variety of tools and techniques available for learning with has never been greater but learning is not just about the formal development your organisation provides for you, it is deeply rooted in your state of mind.

It is not that formal tools and techniques are not useful or insightful; we use them ourselves. It is that they are not the goal. There is a Buddhist saying which roughly summarised says, "do not mistake your finger for the moon". In other words keep in mind that the moon is what you are aiming at, not the thing you are pointing at it with!

In one Establishment organisation we saw a leader at his first meeting with his new team lay his numerous assessments on the table and give a very cogent summary of all of his strengths and weaknesses, so that his new team would have some forewarning of his style. Over the coming months it all played out as predicted. The only surprising aspect was how much that leader desired his people to change their own behaviours to accommodate him, when his own self labelling actually gave him a get-out clause from learning new modes of behaviour himself. Establishment learning at its best.

Challenger leaders point to a different state of mind, one that values purposeful instability, knows that much of our old learning may be out of date and leads us to see everything as our teacher. Tools, training courses, techniques, competencies and psychometrics dominate few of the stories in this book. You don't find the spirit of the Challenger in these places. You find it in people who want to make a difference and who will tear down any barrier to experiencing that, including ones that they have erected within themselves.

In that context, there is good news for all of us, especially those that are well into our lives and careers. You CAN teach old dog new tricks! The field of neuroscience and mindful learning has revealed some very optimistic messages for Challenger leaders about neuroplasticity.[3] It may be a strange word but it accurately sums up what your brain is capable of: "plasticity" essentially means that a structure may be modified by an influence. The research now clearly shows that how you think, what you think and the beliefs you develop really can change your brain. Your mind can change the structure of your brain and you can become an active participant in the process. The brain adapts and restructures in response to repeated patterns by giving more cortical space to those areas that are used more regularly and effectively shrinks areas that are rarely used. This process of constant feedback and alteration in your brain only begins to slow down in your eighth decade.[4] So you have time to begin this process now!

What does this mean for a Challenger Leader? This field of research has rapidly developed over the past ten years. We now know that all of the changes in neurogenesis and sustaining new connections in our brains can be further accelerated by new awareness. As Sharon Begley reported,[5] "neuroplasticity occurs only when the mind is in a particular mental state marked by attention and focus."

Seeing, and learning how to dissolve, habits which are unhelpful to us and those around us, can cause a real change in the way our brains are wired. Old thinking patterns that are more Establishment in nature can literally shrink as they are replaced by attitudes and skills that are more generative of a Challenger leader, IF you learn how to focus your mind and bring attention to what you are thinking and doing.

When you see everything as your teacher and are vulnerable enough to embrace the possibility of looking awkward, unskilled, or in a confused mess for a while, then you are operating as a Challenger would. Your learning can come from anywhere, often when you least expect it; it requires you to be open to your own ignorance and benefit from exploring difficulties and breakdowns together with those you work with.The Challenger intentionally seeks, creates and thrives on those conditions so that they can learn at a faster rate than their competitors.

Getting Stuck In

Inner Work

- What area of learning is hardest for you because of your 'Establishment' mindset?
- What personal strategies have you developed to reduce your learning?
- How do you feel when you are really learning? How often are you feeling this at the moment?
- Which of the following areas do you feel you can and can't change for yourself? Awareness, Interpersonal Skills, Technical Skills, Beliefs, Values, Energy, Purpose.
- How can you accelerate your learning in your current environment?

Outer

- To achieve a Challenger goal, what must you learn to do with spirit?
- How can you coach your team to see the connection between learning and results?
- What form of systemic learning must happen for you and your team to be successful?
- How can you make your learning and your action as a Challenger more aligned?
- Which Challenger pattern of behaviour will most help you achieve your goals?

Your Notes,
Insights and Scribbles

What Good Looks Like

Learning fuels the engine.

- Uses every situation to provide and provoke learning.
- Uses failure as opportunity to learn.
- Seeks every opportunity to get better at what they do.
- Is seen as a thought leader in the team/organisation
- Uses what they don't know as a positive opportunity for stretch and new solutions.

Is a habitual student

- Invests time and energy into their own learning.
- Shows an underlying passion to understand.
- Takes responsibility for their own learning.
- Talks about what they need to do to improve.
- Is relentlessly curious.
- Listens and questions more than answers.
- Is willing to be vulnerable about what they don't know.
- Is confident being ignorant because it is an opportunity to learn.
- Is a role model of inquiry and interest.

Gets beneath the surface to learn.

- Is keen to explore what they and the team don't know and need to learn; asks insightful questions that help identify a way forward.
- Is willing to learn from peers, team and customers.

- Looks for new sources of learning from a wider field of possibilities.
- Creates rich insights into situations and experiences
- Is able to understand what lies beneath issues.
- Provides novel and interesting new ways of looking at things.
- Seeks to understand how things work.
- Shows a willingness to get into the 'messy' detail of issues.

Infects the system with a learning mindset.

- Encourages others to be curious.
- Deliberately takes self and others outside their comfort zone to get a breakthrough in results.
- Encourages others to learn.
- Asks the team what they learnt today.
- Creates the time and conditions for conversation and reflection.
- Sees conversation as the most important tool for finding solution and learning.
- Holds people accountable in equal measure for learning and results.
- Won't let people off the hook who don't seek to learn.
- Encourages learning outside their team.

Creates safe uncertainty and active experimentation.

- Overtly thrives on uncertainty.
- Encourages healthy tension and disagreements to fuel learning.

- Encourages free expression of confusion, fear and pessimism as an important part of learning.
- Doesn't penalise mistakes, rather penalises safe thinking.
- Creates an atmosphere where it is safe to speak up.
- Encourages experimentation and trial and error.
- Is able to turn learning insight into actions.
- Allows solutions to emerge over time.
- Pushes people out of their comfort zone to address real issues.
- Provides just enough support to enable people to take risks.

6 Dance, Prod and Shuffle

Enjoying The Mess

This is about being flexible, agile, adaptive, sensitive and responsive. It is taking what emerges from the instability you have caused, building on it and passing it on. It is improvisational rather than scripted and there is enjoyment in the iteration, mess and confusion. It is creating momentum in yourself and others by moving, pausing and moving again with changes in circumstances. It is collaborative and interdependent, giving others the freedom to act and create, trusting their judgement. It is taking graciously what others offer in the organisation and not seeking to constrain or block. It requires a deep understanding of the rhythms of change in yourself and others, seeing the occasional drama for what it is, treating it compassionately and continuing to keep moving.

Establishment organisations are mostly hierarchical, slow, inflexible in their processes, rigid in their structures and difficult to move. They are often led by a small number of strong individuals who rely on control, power, process and structure to determine the future direction of 'their' organisations. Agreement, stability and consistency are valued.

> *We find ourselves going through a budget round four times a year. I often wonder – what would the founders of our company think about this? Wouldn't they be horrified? (Ian Armstrong, European Marketing, Honda.)*

Stability is built into the Establishment organisation through rigorous processes, review boards, leaders with long experience, many layers of management and a received wisdom on how things are done around here.

> *There is an immutable conflict at work in life and in business, a constant battle between peace and chaos. Neither can be mastered, but both can be influenced. How you go about that is the key to success. (Phil Knight, Founder, Nike.)*

Challenger organisations are more biological than industrial. They need to be adaptive, mobile, open, sensitive to their environment and responsive. Diversity, disagreement, creativity and relationships are valued. That is not to say that no controls are needed. The leadership challenge is that a gentle touch on the controls AND an openness to difference, diversity and disagreement is required. Successful Challengers maintain enough control to manage their business without it suffocating the energy flows that a Challenger Spirit requires to grow.

We wanted to reconnect with and expand this aspect of our organisational DNA. One of the ways we do this is to move away from traditional communication – the top down press releases etc. We are moving towards opening the organisation up to far more transparent and dynamic communication. Information is free; people make up their own stories. So we have been sharing our stories with each other, using the traditional and new vehicles. Chat rooms, Internet fora, blogging, wikis, and conferences. We also sit in an open floor plan, everyone from the CEO down. Visible, accessible and ready to talk to anyone that wants to. We ensure the freedom of information, that it flows and that it moves at a fast pace. The surprise was how much this internal communication improved the external communication with customers, regulators etc. We find that once the ball starts moving it is impossible to stop. The technocrats and bureaucrats get scared and are still trying to stop the flow but they can't, the human will is too strong for them. We decided let's not waste our leadership energy trying to control this communication, it's a myth that we can control it, let's work with it, not against it. (Glenn King, CEO Servco, National Australia Bank.)

Challenger organisations are typically built to be unstable – smaller groups of people that are working under less supervision. Sometimes making up the process as they go along, relying less on exhaustive research and more on instinct. Their conversations are more contentious, intense and passionate.

6.1 Paradox and Performance

> *"The thing about inventing is you have to be both stubborn and flexible, more or less simultaneously. Of course, the hard part is figuring out when to be which!" (Jeff Bezos, Founder, Amazon.)*

Many of the Challenger Leaders we have worked with were in organisations of significant size despite in many cases not being the market leader. Being second, third or fourth in a market didn't mean they were small. They still had a need to emphasise centralisation, structure, process discipline, planning and long-term focus: all aspects of providing a degree of 'certainty' for their organisation. What made the successful ones stand out was that they managed to lead through the paradox of needing certainty and uncertainty at the same time if they were to challenge the Establishment organisations.

As Challenger organisations grapple with the certainty/ uncertainty paradox, leaders find themselves faced with a number of other paradoxes that are connected to it: co-existing states that are not always compatible with each other. In Challenger organisations they are often being asked to be: persistent and adaptive; centrally led and locally led; structured and chaotic; disciplined on process and challenging of process; planned and opportunistic; long term and short term; customer led and leading the market; growing and efficient.

Inevitably organisational leaders have difficulty leading through these paradoxes. Efforts to meet the challenge can give rise to an over emphasis on which side of the paradox is right rather than leading both positions. All too often in Establishment organisations the default positions take on the qualities of either/or, win or lose, top dog or underdog. Challengers find a way to live with paradox rather than getting stuck in it or letting it be a cause of internal conflict.

Howard Schultz, the founder of Starbucks, is one of the most celebrated Challengers in recent corporate history. Recently taking back the reins at Starbucks in order to get the performance back on track has challenged his ability to lead through paradox.

> *"I've had to change my own mentality and thinking," he says. "It's always a fragile balance between creativity and discipline, but it's much more acute than it was in the past."*
>
> *Spend enough time with Schultz, and one thing becomes clear. Despite the recent reversals and reckonings, he still wants it all. Starbucks must be powerful and benevolent, respected and passionate, ubiquitous and imaginative. There is no point telling him that no big corporation, certainly not one with some 16,000 stores in 50 countries, has ever found such a balance. He simply doesn't buy it. Yet he concedes the strain of trying to stay true to his shareholders and his original vision.*[1]

6.2 More Comedy Store, Less Shakespeare

The contrast between improvisational theatre and traditional theatre in some ways reminds us of the contrast between Challenger organisations and Establishment organisations. Traditional theatre follows a standard script with little room for deviation from it. There is an inherent inflexibility built into the form, with repetition, night after night, creating a particular dynamic in the relationships between the cast and the audience. Improvisational theatre has a dramatically different form with the potential for much more uncertainty, diversity and disturbance. And of course this correlates with more risk. So one of the questions in the improvisational form is the same as in Challenger organisations – how can we be both more uncertain and more effective at the same time? The traditional form keeps you focused on an expectation of what is coming next. You know your lines and are thrown into real difficulty if the line offered is not the one you expected. In the improvisational form you have no idea what is coming next, which encourages a stronger focus on the present moment than the past or future moment.

A powerful aspect of the improvisational metaphor is that it teaches you how to keep moving when a situation is particularly ambiguous, complex, pressurised and interconnected. An improvisational scene is an extreme example of an environment that successful Challengers have learned how to thrive in. In both environments you make small changes quickly and then have a high sensitivity towards what happens next so that you can respond and adjust.

> *We started with no strategy, nothing, no research, nothing, no understanding of our competitors, nothing. We borrowed £17k and we started and then we worked with what happened next. There is no glamorous spin to this story. We were simply driven by a belief that it must be possible to do it a little bit better than the guy around the corner. That is still the same. (Julian Metcalfe, Co-founder and CEO, Prêt a Manger.)*

One of the first realisations that hit us in learning about this form is how a competitive mindset is consciously and unconsciously present in most relationships. If this is not brought to the surface and paid attention to then it becomes particularly limiting. In improvisational terms this way of relating is labelled as a block. Your partner makes you an offer that they need you to accept and build on but your competitive mindset generates a block. When you have experienced and watched others do this a few times you notice how poor it makes the performance. The audience of an improvisational theatre scene want you to commit to each other, not to block each other. The Challenger teams we have worked with have realised this and they consciously work with it. The benefit is one of speed and as we recall from an earlier pattern of behaviour: momentum overcomes mass.

The next realisation is that when operating in uncertain or ambiguous environments you can progress more safely and quickly once you have generated some shared meaning together. In an improvisational setting you work together, listening, accepting offers and committing to each other until some shared meaning has been created between you. In theatrical terms this relates to questions of character, relationship between characters, location and ultimate destination of the scene. It fascinates us how positive, bold choices help to establish shared meaning faster than tentative ones. It is easier to respond to a partner who wholeheartedly takes on the character of an elephant drinking a pint in the local bar than one who is someone anonymous walking down the high street!

> *Everything up to the point of commitment had been data analysis from me, I was looking for the data to make the decision for me which of course it never*

can. At the moment I realised my commitment was more compelling than the personal risk then everything changed. My mindset flipped from 'why not?' to 'how?'. My language changed from 'try' to 'will'.

I notice that when leaders are committed people really sense it because commitment leaks out in big and small ways, and so does being uncommitted. Once I was committed, people began to follow. You can smell commitment. (Graham Payne, Managing Director, MBNL.)

In the terms of a Challenger, once you have made some positive, bold choices, created your dream together and engaged people in it, the uncertainty of the environment quickly becomes much easier to navigate.

Thirdly, there is a particular spirit that gets created through the experience of improvisation that provides another parallel to the experiences recounted to us by Challenger leaders. This comes through having to progress with minimal resources, working with whatever becomes available, being interdependent, building on each other's contributions, creating an output in the moment, not knowing what is coming next, enjoying the surprises along the way and the relief at the end. All of this generates a kind of addiction; a quality of wanting more of the same, which, we believe, is a consequence of these conditions. Both the short lived experience of improvisational theatre and the longer experience of leading a Challenger organisation makes you feel more alive to your capability, the relationships you have and what together you might make possible.

If you think about Japan in the 1950s it was a difficult place to be, he (Soichiro Honda) had a view at the time that was far reaching. He was so confident in the development of his motorcycle he decided he would declare his ambition to the world. He runs a newspaper ad that says we are going to win the biggest motorcycle race in the world (which at the time was the Isle of Man TT). He declared his interest and declared it as publicly as he possibly could. Honda ran this as a newspaper ad and then he turns up on the Isle of Wight rather than the Isle of Man! Eventually gets to the Isle of Man, loses every race he enters, takes away machine parts from his competitors, comes home via Germany, can't transport all of his luggage, (so bins some in order that he can get the machine parts home) and then studies everything that his competitors were doing. Honda has now been in TT for 60 years and dominated the thing. With this original ambition of the company's founder he was shouting about something he hadn't achieved...yet. (Ian Armstrong, European Marketing, Honda.)

Finally, in order to be entertaining an improvisational scene usually has introduced at some point a 'tilt' – a source of conflict, a twist that the improvisers have to respond to. Most comedy in an improvisation is the product of a tilt and how it is responded to. We go on in the section on 'Leading Through The Noise' to look at how an unhealthy organisational response to a tilt can derail key initiatives and projects.

We have learned a lot about Challenger cultures from looking at them through the metaphor of Improvisational Theatre. We don't have time to outline all the insights here but if you are interested in further reading we can recommend the writing of some of our teachers: John Cremer,[2] Neil Mullarkey and Keith Johnstone.[3]

6.3 Prodding the Bear

The establishment brand in BA we thought of as 'prodding the bear'. Every time we prodded the bear, he got angry and that was a result for us, it became newsworthy. (Chris Moss, ex-CMO, Virgin Airlines.)

Challengers benefit from prodding the bear, whether the bear is a dominant competitor or an Establishment group culture. The act of prodding in the first place is one way of causing the disturbances we explored through the pattern of Purposeful Instability, creating an environment through which the Establishment Spirit becomes more vulnerable to Challenger Spirit. The second part of prodding the bear is that you inevitably get a reaction whether from the competitor or your internal group culture. The problem is you have no idea when you prod what the reaction is going to be; more often than not the bear surprises you. This is when your capability as a Challenger to dance, prod and shuffle comes into play.

I was at a meeting with a potential client a few weeks ago and they asked me which parts of the work we'd discussed would add the most value. They were rather taken aback by my response of "I don't know". I explained that, in all the organisations that I've worked with, the success of the change and the activity which drive it have never been predictable.

This truth is uncomfortable to many Establishment organisations that prefer certainty and a highly structured approach, even if, as is my belief, that is not how change in organisations ever really works.

At the Establishment end of the continuum, Executive Teams tend to believe that it is enough to declare what you want to happen. And then they get increasingly frustrated as the desired change doesn't happen or doesn't happen fast enough. The Executive Teams of Challenger organisations realize that they have to work through the change with the people involved, responding moment by moment; putting themselves into the pattern of behaviour that they are intending to change. To Dance, Prod and Shuffle through the work they have initiated.

This came to life recently with a Challenger client that wanted to differentiate themselves in their sector by providing a customer experience that was superior to and clearly distinct from their competitors. Through a series of interventions a new customer experience was initiated resulting in a tangible improvement in the customer interaction. In reflecting together on this success we realised how the point of greatest impact was not where they would have originally expected.

The first step included a series of Summits that involved employees and customers exploring and amplifying the best of the current Customer Experience. This resulted in a tangible improvement in the customer interaction. The Summits, however, were not the intervention that made the biggest difference.

Leaders talked to those involved in a different way than they had before. They admitted that they didn't have all the answers and that they needed help in designing the future. This was sometimes difficult for the team and many of the leadership talked about feeling a sense of vulnerability and being exposed in a way that they weren't used to. But it wasn't this that made the biggest difference.

Within a few days of the Summits, members of the frontline teams started acting in ways that hadn't been asked of them. They were being proactive in speaking about and offering services the customer hadn't mentioned; they were talking to customers in a far less formal and more relational manner.

They were taking it upon themselves to apply the spirit and the freedom that had informed the Summit. But it wasn't this that made the biggest difference.

The frontline team members were testing and experimenting in a new way with some anxiety in the background. What would be the reaction to their creative first steps from the leadership team that usually insisted on controlling things very tightly?

With some help and some deliberation, the response of the leadership team was to overcome their own instinctive nervousness and instead, to celebrate this innovation and risk-taking. Including a celebration of experiments that didn't result in an improved customer experience. It was this reaction that made the biggest difference to the change effort.

The organisation now had reason to believe that the change was real and authentic. The scene was set for momentum and a competitive spirit emerged across departments as to who could best improve the customer experience. The change in atmosphere was palpable.

So in summary, what should you consider when embarking on this kind of change? When you make a provocation or intervention are you prepared for what comes back? If it isn't exactly what you expect (or want), how will you react? Which reaction will you choose in order to accelerate the change?

Change happens as you learn to relate differently to the issue at hand. By putting something into the organisation and working with what comes back, the real change happens in your response to their response to your request! Dance, prod and shuffle. (Roger Taylor, Relume)

6.4 Leading Through the Noise

I've learned that it's always better to sit down with people in advance and communicate that we're about to take a different type of journey. Give them the opportunity to enrol emotionally and decide, not right away, whether they wanted to lead, follow or get out of the way. In about 3 months I would do the same again. I would warn them that we were going to make a lot of mistakes; hopefully none of them would be fatal. This was not going to be a circle on a Ferris wheel. This causes anxiety but in my experience it's better in the long run and provides much more fortitude and stamina for the journey. (Clent Richardson, ex VP Worldwide Developer Relations & Solutions Marketing, Apple Inc.)

In an emergent environment which depends on improvisation as a way of moving forward, the easiest way to destroy momentum is simply to stand in the way in some form; for example, by requesting more and more information before being willing to act; or by pointing out what the risks of an action were rather than saying a strong 'yes' or a strong 'no' to it. This expression of lead, follow, or get out of the way encourages people to make an active contribution and to ask themselves where they stand. Being 'in the way' simply isn't an option. Perhaps it would be more accurate to say that being in the way would be tolerated if you had a strong but creative contrary view; however, it would be incumbent to bring that view out it into the open rather than to let people infer that you had a particular view from the way in which you dragged your heels.

This is particularly pertinent when a team or organisation has reached a difficulty on the Challenger path they were travelling. This can manifest as an unexpected turn of events, a loss of performance, reduced levels of sponsorship, disbelief in the cause, new fears or a breakdown in understanding of some kind.

This often generates a dramatic quality of response, with energy, excitement, new possibilities and pace being infected by fault finding, blame, pessimism, loss of energy, distancing and disengagement. At this point of a Challenger journey it is very tempting to either stop (and start again) or reduce the scope of the ambition and deliver a smaller (substantially different) result. The excitement felt at the start of the Challenger project can then be felt all over again with a new project. A new project that inevitably has to begin because the old situation was never resolved, it was just avoided.

The sorts of questions and statements that stimulate this drama have a familiar tone to them once you have seen a few of these situations occurring. Is this the right thing to be doing? Have we got the right focus here before we progress? Is this the right time to be doing this? Are we clear enough? Let's get more clear on this before we progress. Have we enough time to be doing this? We are too busy. Let's prioritise before we progress.

Figure 6.1 Leading Through The Noise.

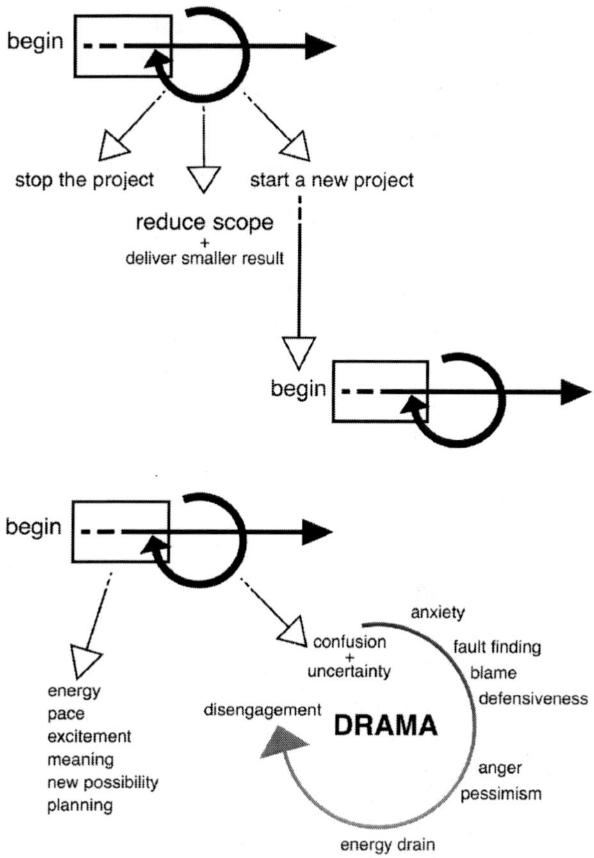

Different people react to this drama in different ways depending on their personal response to the anxiety they are feeling. There are those who exaggerate the pattern, creating more drama, looking for others to blame, defending themselves and lining up behind the most politically powerful force in the situation at the time.

There are those who expect the drama from the very beginning and therefore stay emotionally disengaged from the beginning. They describe this as a way of protecting themselves from the inevitable disappointments to come. This population often contains leaders who have started with the best of intentions and found themselves worn down by the repetitive experience.

There are those who see the drama coming and disengage themselves, focusing on what they do from their comfort zone. This approach can still lead to something being delivered but it is done in an isolated way; hot housing ideas and plans within an area of functional expertise. There is little trust or faith in the possibility of a bigger result being achieved by working together outside of the silo.

Many Establishment organisations have this pattern repeating itself over and over again. They become participants in this drama of starting a new project with lots of excitement, allowing the drama of a difficulty to stop it, sweeping it under the carpet and starting again. There are lots and lots of political effort expended, giving the impression of an organisation that is moving forward, but in reality it is stuck without any traction.

A successful Challenger organisation learns how to expect and predict these moments and develops a capability to dance, prod and shuffle their way through the anxiety and occasional drama. They do not stop or reduce their scope; they flex, fight and invent their way through the difficulty, learning as they go.

One of the Executive Teams we worked with came up with the following principles once they had understood their own dramatic pattern of behaviour. This was their version of dance, prod and shuffle.

- We notice when we are about to repeat our usual pattern and make some new choices.

- Fluctuations, disturbances, imbalances, uncertainties are seen as sources of creativity rather than as a loss of control that will damage us.
- We recognise our individual contributions to the beginning of the drama or its continuation.
- We find a way of experiencing the drama and converting its energy into a productive one that can be used for learning.
- We change our relationship to breakdowns, seeing them as opportunities for breakthroughs rather than opportunities to slow down or stop.
- We value telling each other our truths as we see them. We care enough about each other to do so.

The Practice Ground

If initial efforts in causing a shift are not deemed successful enough, Establishment leaders will default their change strategy to a programme, more structure, mandatory tasks, objectives and greater 'business focus'. If they don't like the way certain parts of the organisation are dragging their feet or seeming to work against the goal, they develop an aversion to those actions and those people. The trouble with aversion in this context is that it very quickly develops into separation, distancing and blame. When these start to show up in your leadership discourse you know your challenger behaviour and intentions are being downgraded. You are defaulting to the establishment way of dealing with difficulty, surprise, disturbance or dissent when it comes back at you.

What lies at the heart of this pattern of behaviour is a commitment to work with everything that comes at you, even if it is not the way you want it to be. In Buddhist practice we sometimes describe this as "roll it all in". We stay up close and personal to everything as it presents itself, even the parts of our thinking or emotions that we would rather we didn't have; we don't suppress anything and we don't avoid anything by occupying ourselves with thoughts and feelings that are more acceptable to us. We don't achieve growth and change by doing that. If we avoid these feelings in others, or ourselves, they simply stay there waiting for a moment to arise again. If we try to suppress them, they grow in energy as a form of resistance to our efforts and seem to trip us up under pressure.

In Challenger leadership terms we do not distance ourselves from difficulty, we come up alongside it; we even waltz with it if we can! We don't expect to dictate a change in mindset or understanding, we accept that we will have to keep returning to prod, shuffle and be light footed.

This is not a failure although it may feel that way to those who don't like the natural messiness of this approach. It's not about being a patient saint, it's about staying close to people who try to defend the establishment or thwart your ambition. It's also about welcoming and building on the unintended consequences of your initial actions. It is healthier and more transforming to keep unexpected responses to your ambition surfaced and part of the total leadership discourse, than to suppress them, attempt to gloss over them or repress them with sanctions. When this happens as it frequently does in Establishment organisations it appears to divert a lot of the energy and life-blood away from the ambition into dissention and avoidance. It is costly in terms of money and service; it kills creative energy and slows things down.

At the centre of this practice ground are Challenger leaders learning to overcome the more primal sensations that are mediated by the limbic area of the brain. Our fight, flight, and freeze responses are activated whenever we sense danger. The limbic system in our brain is constantly assessing whether the world, people or issues are safe for us. When we encounter difficulty, or resistance or aggression in others that we are trying to lead, the limbic system stands ready to protect us. Regulating your own emotional reactions and attuning to the intentions and feelings of others to minimise the effects of this activation is critical.

A characteristic of people who work at this practice is their ability to trust emergence. They are prepared to open their minds to possibilities that emerge from the field in which they are operating, rather than assuming that everything of value arises purely from planning. Ideas and opportunities seem to flow though them a little more easily because they are spacious on the inside even in times of heightened stress. This quality of spaciousness is an example of the mind working the brain to everyone's advantage.

If all of this sounds a little too good to be true to you, perhaps it is time to think of all the experiences you have encountered where these skills and attitudes have not been present. And perhaps more importantly what the human and commercial costs are of not having senior leaders in businesses with these kinds of skills. What do blame, control, emotional outbursts, protectionism and avoidance cause in our workplaces?

You can strengthen and deepen yourself as a Challenger leader if you manage to stay close to those who offer you an unexpected response to your intentions. Even resistance and dissent taste better to you if you are intimate with them. It is more agile and invigorating to adopt this approach, than the dead formulas of Establishment change.

Getting Stuck In

Inner Work

- How do you manage strong emotions when you don't get your own way?
- What is your instinctive view about resistance, and how is this helping or hindering you?
- What types of situations are invoking your avoidance?
- How do you keep your energy refreshed?
- How can you moderate your reactions to keep yourself on track?

Outer Work

- What 'yes buts' are you encountering?
- How much time are you devoting to breakthrough thinking?
- What strategies do you have for leading through the noise?
- How do you know you are making an impact?
- How are you staying light on your feet and keeping things moving?

Your Notes, Insights and Scribbles

What Good Looks Like

Displays a fleetness of foot.

- Acts with speed and decisiveness.
- Is able to respond quickly and effectively in complex and ambiguous situations.
- Is able to make the best use of a situation when things haven't gone as expected.
- Is opportunistic rather than sticking rigidly to a plan.
- Holds firm to a underlying purpose.
- Is enthusiastic about new developments.
- Relies on instinct not exhaustive research.
- Balances the short and the long term.

Keeps things in perpetual motion.

- Restlessness.
- Creates pauses to cause just as much momentum as a push.
- Continually building on things.
- Treating changes in circumstance as a opportunity to improve.
- Staying the course.
- Setbacks don't dent enthusiasm.
- Injects energy into challenges.
- Maintains energy in the face of setbacks.
- Commits swiftly to actions and doesn't get held up.

Helps others learn how to dance, prod and shuffle.

- Coaches others in how to be flexible and adapt.
- Shares stories about success and failure to move things forward.

Can improvise and adapt.

- Is sensitive to what is happening in the team / organisation environment.
- Is able to respond effectively when things get messy.
- Takes on challenges with enthusiasm.
- Takes the best from all situations.
- Is able to take advantage of new situations.
- Builds on the ideas of others.
- Shows a willingness to experiment.
- Uses every recourse at their disposal.
- Doesn't let organisation boundaries and processes get in the way.
- Make good calls with all the information.

Gives freedom to others to act, adapt and sit at the dynamic edge of chaos.

- Gives people trust and freedom to act independently.
- Happy to hear others using their language and ideas as a source of infection rather than ownership.
- Allows people to use their judgement and doesn't second guess.
- Is patient to see what emerges.
- Encourages people to trust and respect others effort.

- Frees up people to act decisively in the face of resistance.
- Tackles head on negative thinking. Doesn't allow dissention to spread.
- Is willing to rely on others.
- Develops strong relationships at all levels that encourage experimentation.
- Breaks down boundaries for people in order to move things forward.
- Takes risk on people to get the best out of them.

7 Being the Face on the Dartboard

Nurturing Bouncebackability

This is about resilience as distinct from endurance. It is about having a strong core that doesn't get compromised by a desire for pragmatism, recognition and reward. It is being comfortable taking action and doing things that will be unpopular. It is managing your energy so that your passion and commitment don't exhaust you. It is about understanding the nature of continuous stress and using a well-developed set of practices to sustain yourself. It is dealing with feelings of anger, resentment, sadness and guilt directed towards you. It is about having an awareness of how you sabotage yourself and some strategies for working through this. It is avoiding getting trapped in a defensive or victim mentality and blaming others. It is using compassion for yourself and others as a source of resilience. It is being able to be emotionally regulated in tough circumstances. It is helping the people around you stay healthy and effective in difficult circumstances.

Good or bad, I am making some seismic changes around here and people do have my face on a dartboard. I can show you the e-mails but the reality is we are going to end up in a better place. But you have got to be willing to take the heat, if not, you are not able to be a Challenger. Every day you are encouraging people to go into more difficult places. It is not always appreciated; sometimes it creates an angry response. (Graham Neale, SVP Nutritional Healthcare Future Group, GlaxoSmithKline.)

7.1 Creating, Using and Containing Anxiety

The type of leadership that is needed in a Challenger strategy has its basis in high personal resilience, collaboration and enough resonance with people to galvanize them to release more energy and pace. These leaders are particularly good at working at the interface between unfreezing people and processes and containing the anxiety that inevitably follows from doing that. They have a willingness to move towards problems and difficulty, are compassionate towards others and have developed an inner stability in the face of stressful circumstances.

> *We create instability in environments that don't like it, that's what Challenger leaders do. You just have to keep falling out, generate the tension in the group and then hold it there. (Mark Palmer, Global Brand Director, Green and Blacks.)*

Those that are successful seem to have some practices that help them work with their own anxiety. Challengers wouldn't be human if they didn't feel anxious about some of the instability in their environment. What marks them out is that they are able to recover from and use their anxiety in helpful ways. They also work at containing the anxiety of the people they are working with so that it can be used productively and doesn't degenerate into a drama.

In the heat of instability a Challenger's resilience enables them to be flexible and free of internal constraint. They occupy the middle ground of the matrix described in the chapter on Purposeful Instability. Not rigid, dull and stuck on the one hand or chaotic, fragmented, explosive and unpredictable on the other.

7.2 The Resilience of the Challenger

> *It's a combination of discovery and heroics that I get subsumed by. (Kevin Page, General Manager, National Australia Bank.)*

> *Once you make this commitment, you then have to think what is the next thing? And the next thing? And the next thing? How do you maintain that momentum, keep moving yourselves forward? That is where the exhaustion of leading a Challenger organisation comes into play, how do you maintain that momentum, keep engaging the employee base and manage the expectations of multiple stakeholders? You have set a new ambition, a new baseline; this is an incredible energy requirement for individuals and the organisation as a whole to live up to. (Phil Thomson, SVP Global Communications, GlaxoSmithKline.)*

You don't have to spend long in the Challenger space to realise that what is really being asked of you as an individual is something that requires you to be willing to dig very deep within yourself again and again. A sort of perpetual alertness to keep pushing the boundaries of your own comfort zone and that of others to deliver the big result, shake up the market or to change the playing field on which your competitors participate. In some cases the most challenging work for leaders in this space is to slow things down, remain in the ambiguity, deliberately disrupt and disturb habitual patterns of business behaviour to create the conditions for something new to emerge. This kind of action takes strength, courage and self-efficacy.

> *Asked to describe his personality, he comes up with a list of defects headed by 'obstinacy'. Such self-deprecation is very English and judged by English cultural norms reflects confidence rather than insecurity. No one would ever have heard of James Dyson were it not for his huge belief in his own vision.*[1]

As a Challenger, you are bound to draw criticism towards you. When you step out you also invoke the opinions of others. If the work takes longer than others are comfortable with, you can find yourself in the heat of people's fears and anxieties and for most of us that is a very tough place to stand. It is then that you need what Peter Kramer describes as "Bouncebackability"!![2]

We love that word for the audacity it shows with the English language, but mostly because it seems to capture that special quality about resilience that speaks of elasticity, leaping back into life after a period of compression, the ability to recover readily and begin again.

7.3 Self Sabotage

Creating a Challenger culture requires leaders to be able to contain their own anxiety in response to the challenge they are creating in the organisation. If you can't handle your own anxiety you will end up sabotaging yourself and your efforts.

The very experience of creating instability can cause all kinds of strong personal emotions – confusion, anger, fear, pessimism, and doubt. These emotions are often suppressed, denied or avoided. We imagine that if we were to allow them free expression that we would cause a personal or relational breakdown of some kind. Those who challenge the organisational status quo successfully have learned what the source of these emotions are, how they are triggered and how they can work through them effectively.

They stop being something to avoid and become something to welcome, a sign that there is a potential breakthrough in the air.

> *One of the fatal flaws stopping me from leading the organisation to achieving greater things was this intensity of wanting to be liked (more than valued if I am really honest). Wanting to be warmly invited in as opposed to just being accepted because of my position as the regional President, there to do a quarterly review or whatever the activity at the time was. And I realised what a huge barrier that was to me being at my best and others being at their best. I took on a leadership stand, a desire to shift something in my leadership, which was expressed as 'I care so much, I don't care'. I care deeply about the*

people in my organisation but actually it was a bit fraudulent I came to realise because if I really cared, I wouldn't have been holding back on some of the judgements, some of the feelings, some of the observations, or sharing them in a sugar-coated way. If I really cared about the individual I would want them to be the best that they could be and would take myself out of the equation. I was caring more about me and what they thought of me than I was about them. (Stuart Fletcher, President of International, Diageo.)

There are many ways of thinking about personal anxiety, here is one that is easily understood and applied by organisational Challengers that we have worked with.

In transactional analysis theory, negative restrictive messages we receive from early authority figures may generate within us forms of equally restrictive behaviour called 'Drivers'.[3] Drivers contain socially acceptable moral judgments and value statements – superficially, driver behaviour looks good.

There are five groupings of drivers: please others, be strong, be perfect, try hard, and hurry up. A response to one of these internal directives will please the historical 'parent' in us (or our own 'conscience') and so result in good feelings. When these are repeated, the person comes to assume 'I'm okay if…', for instance, 'I'm okay, if I please others'. Identification with such an assumption can eventually become exclusive in the sense 'I'm okay **only** if I please others.' This is where a source of our personal sabotage comes from.

The implication behind each driver demonstrates the negative aspect and restrictive message initially internalised by the individual:

- Please others – you must not be yourself
- Be Strong – don't allow yourself any feelings (especially involving 'weakness')
- Be Perfect – whatever you do isn't good enough
- Try Hard – because you won't succeed
- Hurry Up – you will never be on time

In organisational life, we learn to use emotional energy in driver behaviour to gain the recognition or approval of others. To some extent this is a means of coping with the world around us, rather than giving ourselves permission to have feelings, please ourselves, take our time, make mistakes sometimes and above all, be authentic and be ourselves.

When creating a successful Challenger culture leaders have learned to identify and understand when their primary driver has the potential to sabotage their efforts. They are able to short circuit their conditioned brain's wiring even if only for a short time so that the Challenger Project has a chance to survive the early days when it is most likely to be rejected or shut down. There is a level of insight developed into knowing when their driver is serving them and when too much energy put into it is a way of reducing their anxiety at the expense of their leadership.

7.4 Valley of Lost Hope

As if all of this wasn't testing enough there is another part of the Challenger journey that adds to the need for resilience. Every organisation and leader that we have worked with or interviewed about their journey has described at least one moment when they and their teams came close to losing hope and giving up. A time when fear, confusion, self-doubt, pessimism, fragmentation and some pain expressed itself.

It helps us to think of this time as not only unavoidable but also critical if a Challenger's aspirations are to be realised. Every transformation of a team, function, organisation or sector brings with it a moment when the past has to be broken away from while the future state is not sufficiently visible or well formed to give you a sense of security that you are heading in the right direction.

There is usually some kind of deal with the devil set up in these moments. Be safe, give up your dream and return to what you have known. Or take the easy route and don't explore the sources of pessimism or hopelessness. If you run fast enough you think you might avoid them or that they will go away.

In these moments the resilience of the Challenger to their own and other peoples' anxiety is paramount – at this stage it is worth making a distinction between resilience and endurance.

7.5 Resilience not Endurance

In Buddhism there is a very helpful idea that is referred to as the 'near enemy'. In it we are able to see that even admirable qualities like resilience can be easily confused with something else. It looks roughly the same, we can use similar words to describe it and yet it has a profoundly different effect on others and ourselves. We think that the near enemy of resilience is Endurance.

We should begin by saying that there is nothing, absolutely nothing wrong with endurance. Our history is littered with inspiring examples of people who have endured extraordinary hardship and survived. We can often endure much more than we think we can.

However in the more common context of organisations, those leaders we coach who sometimes think they are resilient have actually fallen into the trap of enduring situations, cultures and practices which are frankly deadening to the spirit of energy and accomplishment. We actually learn to endure all sorts of subtle things in organisations; small things, which over time build up to a wall that desensitises us to what a lively, creative, passionate and potent organisation could really be like. And we go on to tell ourselves that our survival in such an organisation in a leadership position is actually an example of how resilient we are, without realising that as the years roll by bits of our original enthusiasm, our driving energy, our deep desire to do the right thing have been eroded by the fact that we have survived so many changes.

That is why endurance is the near enemy of resilience. It feels good to have endurance, but it can become the goal in itself. If resilience is lively, challenging, bouncy and full of flexibility; endurance is characterized by stiffness, survival, cutting off from oneself to get through it. That is not the act of a Challenger Leader; it is the act of someone dominated by the need to survive and to cling on.

Several years ago we sat in front of a very talented man who was a senior leader. It was late on a Friday night in his office which had a panoramic view over London. He was wealthy and he had definitely "made it". He was an image of serenity; despite the intense pressures of his work nothing ever seemed to faze him. He went from bigger job to bigger job. He was dissatisfied with the culture he worked in, but he prided himself on being able to not let it affect him. On that evening he finally reached his limit. He sat with his head in his hands and shook. The price he had had to pay was just too much and all his well-practiced endurance that was so applauded by the organisation, and had won him so many appreciative bonuses, finally broke down.

He had endured yes, but he was not resilient. His own story to recovery was long and painful and illustrated to us how confusing endurance for resilience can be a very costly mistake. He had become a fortress; if you are going to be a successful Challenger leader you need to become a river. You need to be able to flow with the currents and not cling to the sides.

7.6 Strong Back, Soft Front

The great news is that you can learn to become more resilient. Instead of just listening to inspiring stories from people who have led extraordinary lives, you can actually increase your own levels of resilience. Neuroscientists now know enough about the brain to see that with focussed attention we can change the neural pathways that have built up over time into rigid patterns and replace them with synaptic connections that increase our flexibility, our resilience and our emotional intelligence. And as these are biological models they transcend issues of history, culture, age and gender. The fact is that whoever you are, whatever age you are and whatever your life experience to date, you can alter the way your brain and your nervous system respond to stressors and increase your zone of resilience.

Challengers learn to have what we think of as ‘a strong back and a soft front’ when they are leading. By that we really mean that they can continue to carry a load and at the same time they are open to what is arising around them, they are staying close to their people and they are right in the heat of all the emotions and opinions that naturally arise when they want to disrupt something comfortable or familiar. Challenger leaders don’t just KNOW ABOUT change, they themselves are EMBODIMENTS of change as they experience it in themselves and can articulate what is going on.

Here is a taster of some of the things that Challenger Leaders have worked out and then made work for them:

- Recognizing the conditions they think they need to lead successfully and realizing they can lead without conditions!
- Understanding their stress reactions and how to invoke the parasympathetic nervous system back into play to discharge stress more frequently
- Distinguishing their patterns of rigidity and what motivates that in them (stifling the Challenger spirit)
- Keeping the mind calm in very activating situations
- Increasing their ‘bottom up’ creative thinking and reducing their ‘top down’ habitual thinking and reactions
- Valuing impermanence and the opportunities it presents
- Increasing their resonance with others to collaborate on Challenger work

- Increasing their connection to their own purpose to sustain them
- Learning the value of the present moment
- Saying no to nothing – learning from all available sources
- Reducing attachments to habitual ways and behaviour
- Tracking emergence with ease
- Bringing all aspects of the self as a leader into play: commercial, technical, psychological and somatic

We think of all of these things as practices because that word contains all the flavours you need to understand the spirit of a Challenger leader. We never see the task as completed, we let go of our personal importance and yet we value ourselves enough to give good quality attention to practicing on a daily basis to keep ourselves mentally supple and emotionally flowing.

We can learn to be more resilient and in making that commitment we can grow more than we expected.

7.7 The Compassionate Challenger

Compassion may seem a strange word to use in a business setting. For most of us a word like this probably resides more easily in charitable endeavours, within our own families and at moments when we, or others face extreme tragedy. At those times we are brought into a sharp relationship with how others are suffering and how we sense a certain desire to empathise or even take action to alleviate the suffering of others.

Yet after years of working in some of the most successful Challenger businesses, it seems to us that it is time the words 'business' and 'compassion' started to develop a more intimate relationship with each other.

Compassion is a quality of connection with others that is not based on our personal preferences. It does not rely on us having likes or dislikes, a stronger sense of affinity for certain people or a feeling of alignment with their goals. It arises in us out of a realisation that regardless of difference we are very closely connected to each other. In fact so closely connected that underneath all of our behavioural traits and idiosyncrasies, we all desire to be happy and to be well.

However it is much easier for us to assume that people have different needs, motivations and goals from our own. It is much easier for us to assume that different means less capable. We do this because we have a deeply ingrained and mistaken belief that we are actually separate. Leadership development has never really woken up to this idea. In fact it has focussed more on creating a sense of separation and the development of the leader's ego as a necessary part of developing a leadership credo. In other words we have focussed more on differentiation rather than connection. When you think of yourselves as separate moving parts of a machine, the need for compassion towards each other rarely arises.

In Establishment businesses a lack of compassion can manifest itself in the following ways:

- Blaming
- Gossiping

- Projecting
- Judging and criticising
- Avoiding
- Delaying

When compassion is lacking people leap to blame others for a breakdown in results. In doing so they make assumptions about the capability, motivations and agendas of others and these are always less favourable than their own self-evaluation would be. Over time these dynamics become part of a business culture that passes from one person to another until it forms part of the normal fabric of conversation. Business planning, projects and discussions become infected with some of the activities outlined above causing a reduction in what is possible at the strategic and people level.

It takes longer to get traction on important business opportunities; requests for information are met with indignation or delay; and when difficulties arise, as they inevitably do, it takes much longer to get to the heart of issues as they are clouded by personal judgements and negative projections. (If we labelled these sales and marketing, or group centre and business unit, or regional office and country business, we think you will understand).

In this environment talented executives with very demanding roles give 120% to the work and still live with an inner knowing feeling that they are not good enough. Despite the fact that they have little recovery time and are on the edge of their comfort zone most of the time, their inner dialogue is often harsh and censorial. They live in a state of inner arousal about their performance or lack of it, and spend their time vigilantly trying to avoid disappointing others.

These scenarios have been part of our experience in Establishment and Challenger organisations and we have witnessed the human and the business costs of each. So when we work with Challenger teams, one of the most significant areas of focus is to bring people back into relationship with each other. When you are in relationship your sense of compassion is more easily activated because you feel connected. When you feel connected to another you naturally feel more interested in them and how they are. You have a desire to solve problems, listen to perspectives and feel as others do. Compassion in business makes sense, and in Challenger businesses is a key source of resilience when causing purposeful instability.

7.8 Not Numbing Out, not Rescuing

It is worth taking a moment to explore two states that sit alongside compassion and regularly trip us up.

Familiarity with people and their circumstances can cause us to become numb to them. This is also true of our own inner state of compassion towards ourselves. We just stop seeing what is there, feeling in relationship and being sensitive to the fact that we are all connected. Work pressure, hierarchies, competition and reduced resources can all contribute to a sense of simply not seeing what is in front of you every day.

Over time we simply numb out. This can also happen when what we feel we have to accomplish may cause others distress or disturbance and rather than confront the consequences of our actions we act as if we are numb to them. We separate ourselves from others and this allows us to take actions that we could not feel easy with if we were more closely connected.

Examples of this pitfall reveal themselves on a spectrum that starts with avoiding a colleague who is being made redundant and takes us all the way to polluting rivers in Nigeria in a region where the press have no access to report what is going on. Numbing out can have serious consequences.

It is not by accident that HR professionals in business can suffer from compassion fatigue as they simply get into a frozen state of numbing out after dealing with mass redundancies. Before you wonder whether you have compassion fatigue yourself it is worth reflecting on the fact that the majority of us who work in organisations are less likely to develop compassion fatigue because we have not done enough to develop a compassionate mindset in the first place.

The second pitfall is something we often mistake as compassion, namely rescuing. We rescue people when their situation activates something unpleasant in us and we want the feeling to come to an end. In other words we sort someone else out so that we don't have to experience an unpleasant state inside ourselves. Our own inner distress gets activated and the only way we can make it stop is to rescue the other.

While these actions may look like kindness, they are coupled with an overly controlling energy and too much investment in the outcome being a certain way. Most of the time we are unaware that we are doing it because we do not have enough self awareness to see that what prompts our action is not compassion for the suffering of another, but actually an avoidance of our own!

In business this type of action can be disempowering, lead to feelings of resentment and the creation of heroics. Every time we engage in actions like this mistaking them for compassion, relationships are diminished not enhanced.

Compassion is based on WE. The other two pitfalls arise when we see ourselves as separate from others as if there is I – YOU, or even worse I – IT. History is littered with the examples of I – YOU degrading into I – IT. In business terms strategic partnerships, senior teams and customer service all suffer from a deep lack of WE in the minds of those responsible.

The Practice Ground

Challenger resilience in this field is only acquired by both the persistent development of inner depth and application of outer strength. Establishment leadership development has got better over the years at this but has very far to go, particularly as its aim is to maintain an establishment mindset, not disrupt it.

Depth is really associated with inner work, and as long as you are breathing you have an inner life that needs stretching and facilitating and has the capacity for change.

We don't meet shallow Challenger leaders. They are people who think deeply about work, the purpose of it, what role it plays in our society and how they can cause themselves and others to break the bonds that hold our establishment thinking to do extraordinary things. They are not philosophers in the conventional sense but they have done enough work on themselves to stop being a block to emergence, ambiguity, ambition and compassion in the face of huge pressures and stresses. They keep mining for more within themselves so that when the work throws up another strong challenge, they can step up in the face of it, without defaulting to the old paradigms of control, separation and defensiveness.

We don't meet weak Challenger leaders. They are people who have a very refined way of articulating and embodying what it means to be strong. Strength is really associated with outer work, or at least that is how Challenger strength manifests itself. We strengthen ourselves through trials, by encountering or creating situations that test us and then learning to participate in them without defaulting to establishment behaviours. Each time the demands get beyond us, our commitment to the inner work reveals its purpose, as we are able to draw on our internal resources and relish the idea of being on the edge. We do not acquire physical strength without exercising muscles and we do not acquire Challenger strength without walking through trials. It is difficult for a purpose and rightly so. Difficulty IS the territory, not just part of it. If we can learn to accept that, we can move towards difficulty, rather than develop an aversion to it just because we are getting older, more senior or more outwardly successful.

The most illuminating area of research in the field of resilience is focusing on the body mind continuum. Looking at the intimate relationship between our minds, our brain physiology and our bodies. We have worked with a number of Challenger leaders to teach them more about their personal zone of resilience, how they can expand it, take care of it and bring themselves back into a sense of regulation when they feel as if they are moving beyond what feels workable. As most of the work of Challenger leaders involves a strong challenge to Establishment organisations, it is hardly surprising that this pattern of behaviour should be so important to gain mastery in.

This is extremely important to any Challenger leader facing a significant stretch in their zone of resilience. These periods of being the face on the dartboard can go on for undetermined periods of time. They can be tough on leaders and their teams and often they can drain hope and determination. Given that there is some danger in simply maintaining a state of self-harming endurance, a new way needs to be found.

Our autonomic nervous system is divided into two parts: the sympathetic nervous system deals with our stress reactions, releasing chemicals into our bodies and getting us ready to react to anything our limbic system deems as unsafe by fight, flight or freeze; the other part is called the parasympathetic nervous system and is often referred to as the rest and digest system. When this system is ascendant in our bodies we may spontaneously yawn, or hear our stomachs rumbling! As this is our autonomic nervous system we cannot directly control it. This part of our experience responds to certain conditions invoking it into play.

The ability to engage your parasympathetic nervous system when the sympathetic cycle has been extended for too long a period of time is critical to the development of resilience. We think of this skill as somatic awareness and we owe a lot of our understanding about this to the work of the Trauma Resource Institute.[4]

By somatic awareness we mean getting attuned to what happens in your body and valuing it as really useful data about how activated you are becoming and what you need to do to achieve regulation again. You don't have to be a psychologist to do this because you don't have to interpret what is happening to you; you just have to notice what is happening. For example, you might be preparing for a conversation with a group that you know are deeply upset by your plans. With awareness, you can notice that your chest feels tight, your stomach is turning a little and your heart rate has gone up. In other words just by imagining talking to that group your limbic system has started its work.

If this state continues for an extended period of time you will find yourself operating outside your zone of resilience for longer than you feel able to manage comfortably. You only have to examine what it means to be a Challenger to know that you are likely to encounter being outside your zone of resilience, on the basis that if you are not experiencing that, you probably aren't being a Challenger in the true sense.

So the aim is twofold: firstly you learn to bring your inner state back into regulation when faced with being the face on the dartboard, and secondly as you do this you actually widen your own personal resilience zone to be able to handle people and their anxiety strategies without causing disruption to your mind or your heart.

The more you use the approaches in this book the wider your zone will be. In addition many Challengers we have interviewed in this research have approaches that they regularly rely on to bring themselves back into a regulated state. They included meditation, physical exercise, visualisation exercises, reconnection with nature, spiritual/religious practices, dancing, singing, yoga and conversations with trusted confidants.

One of the approaches that we offer people to help them manage their own inner state on an ongoing basis is very simple and almost instantaneous. We simply ask people to imagine an activity, a place or an experience where they have felt strong, comfortable and happy. They can choose anything. Then we ask them to intensify the image so that colours, smells, conversations, images are as strong in their imagination as they can be. Once they have it fixed in their mind we ask them to notice what is going on in the body.

Typically what happens is that the body has reacted very quickly to the mental imaging and the parasympathetic nervous system starts to come on line in response to it. This 'rest and digest' sensation takes you back within your resilience zone, regulates your emotions and rebalances your state in seconds. People notice a slowing of the heart rate, a gurgling in the stomach and deeper breaths.

Being a Challenger means being the face on the dart-board. If we think of our bodies as physiological containers for our own stress reactions, if we learn how to look after them, then hopefully in the long run it means that we won't be suffering for it.

Getting Stuck In

Inner Work

- How is your ego coping with the ups and downs?
- Where are you seeking appreciation?
- How are you managing your own anxiety?
- What practices are you using to maintain your resilience?
- Where is sabotage revealing itself to you?

Outer Work

- How are you helping your team with their resilience?
- How are you minimising dramatic conversations about difficult relationships?
- What are you doing to bring more emotional regulation to the team?
- How are you encouraging those around you to listen to dissent and criticism as a source of learning?

Your Notes,
Insights and Scribbles

What Good Looks Like

Inner and outer belief that can be stirred but not shaken.

- Displays an unshakeable belief behind their own convictions.
- Is happy to be perceived as unpopular for the benefit of the business.
- Doesn't hide away when things get tough – walks the floor.
- Is emotionally regulated in difficult circumstances.
- Comfortable doing things that will be perceived as unpopular.
- Is able understand and manage their own stress.
- Is highly confident and optimistic about the future.
- Keeps a sense of perspective when things get difficult.

Holds true to their beliefs and values.

- Sticks their neck out to defend what they believe is right.
- Is unshakeably authentic.
- Tenacious.
- Say what they believe regardless of political implications.
- Is prepared to make tough calls.
- Doesn't play it safe.
- Doesn't take the easy way out.
- Is prepared to say what they mean with honesty.

- Tackles anger head on.
- Steers away from safety for the benefit of the business.
- Defends what they believe is right.

Resilient and durable.

- Displays an understanding about continuous stress and knows how to reduce it.
- Maintains energy in tough situations.
- Balances effort with the need to recover in themselves and others.
- Avoids getting trapped in a defensive or victim mentality.
- Will carry on in the face of resistance.
- Won't let people hold them back.
- See setbacks as new opportunities.
- Keeps a balanced life style during times of extreme workload and encourages team to do the same.
- Can cause the team to have fun and feel good about themselves in times of setback.

Ceaselessly confident in taking action and helping others to do the same.

- Takes decisions without asking permission.
- Past failure doesn't stop them taking action and moving forward.
- Stands by decisions in the face of resistance.
- Encourages others to take decisions.
- Protects people from interference.

Helping others to learn how to stay resilient.

- Embraces anxiety positively in themselves and their people.
- Uses compassion towards self and others as a source of resilience.
- Can utilise an understanding of recovery for self and team.
- Looks to what is making people apprehensive as a source of inspiration.
- Encourages people to move into the unknown.
- Looks to what worries themselves and others to uncover breakthroughs.
- Is confident not giving people all the answers and instead keeps searching for the right questions to ask.
- Can create resources in self and others to increase the zone of resilience when under pressure.
- Is generous with praise and recognition even when things aren't going well.
- Defends and protects people who have stuck their neck out.

Dealing with defensiveness and anger effectively.

- Doesn't blame others for positive action even if unsure of the outcome.
- Is truthful about disagreeing.
- Is able to build strong relationships with those who disagree.
- Does not harbour resentments.
- Compassionate about diverse views and opposition.
- Is able to deal with feelings of anger, sadness and guilt directed toward them.

8 Growing old Disgracefully

Staying lean and hungry

This is about not seeing past success as a resting place but instead seeing future potential as a more compelling conversation. It is about looking for future learning from unconventional sources and being willing to keep connected to young people, societal change and emergent trends. It is refreshing one's purpose commensurate with life stage and future challenges, and mentoring others to become Challengers. This is about your next test or trial, actively working with the places and ideas that scare you, observing what you are resistant to and eating it for breakfast! Staying lean and hungry requires an understanding of any hidden mindsets about age, success, reward, positional power and retirement. It is noticing any imbalance between reflection on past success and future dreams and doing something about it.

As a Challenger we have always thought of ourselves as the 'punk on the high street'. As we mature and continue our successful growth trajectory the focus is to grow old disgracefully, otherwise we will end up becoming Levis. (Bob Bayman, Shopping Experience Director, Diesel Jeans)

The hardest thing about being a successful Challenger is to maintain your organisation's spirit once real success has been achieved. One of the greatest hazards of being a Challenger seems to be success. Success brings with it a change in some of the adversarial conditions that many Challengers thrive on.

> *I think you have to be a bit paranoid when you are finally number one, a lot of what got you to number one is not enough to keep you there. We lost some of our sharpness and edge, complacency had set in. We ended up changing our leadership team quite significantly, three new board members out of six, it was a symbol for the organisation that we were not going to stand still. (Robert Higginson, Managing Director, Warburtons.)*

Complacency is dangerous precisely because Challengers must have momentum. Both the actual momentum of performance and the momentum that comes from the customer perceiving that the Challenger is the organisation to watch, the one that is making the most innovative moves in the market. The reason most Challengers lose momentum is that they fail to realise that they have to change in order to remain the same.[1]

This complacency can set in at any time. Just because a Challenger has been successful in the past gives no guarantees for the future.

Despite historical success at reinventing itself through a series of forms - paper to rubber to electricity to cables to electronics and finally telecommunications – Nokia has struggled recently against Challengers who are taking share at the low cost and premium ends of a device and infrastructure market it owns. Nokia have a strategy to provide functionality that is closer to their competitors and a desire to move from being a hardware provider to establishing stronger relationships with their customers through provision of services. Despite their best efforts the business can't create sufficient pace in its software development to support the strategy. Delay after delay and initiative after initiative suggests a loss of the once present Challenger spirit.

8.1 Success and Acquisition

One of the consequences of success as a Challenger is that you can become an acquisition target of an Establishment organisation that wants to benefit from your spirit. Increasingly Establishment organisations are defaulting to treating Challengers as innovation centres that can be purchased. Historically, this has not been a particularly successful strategy, as the acquisition also needed to bring with it 'synergy savings'. These savings are partly achieved through delivering consistent processes and ways of working between the two organisations that in a short period of time kills the Challenger culture and much of the value that was being purchased. At best the Challenger now turns into solely a cash generator rather than an also being an innovation centre.

Establishment organisations are increasingly waking up to this value destruction, with some of them having more success recently. Rather than buying them and integrating them into an Establishment culture (thereby killing what was wanted in the first place), they contract that the Challenger will be left alone to get on with what they do best. This often involves a deliberate arms length distancing in terms of day-to-day operations.

This successful philosophy also plays through into the setting up of new Challenger business units within an Establishment set up.

> *In our mobile advertising business we are going in and acting as a challenger in a media space that is dominated by large online players such as Google. We took a bold decision in setting that business unit up that we would lease separate premises in the heart of advertising land. This has had a massive impact. They have a buzz, energy and a sales focus. Their office culture inside is very different to our headquarters where we have incubated a number of our other start-ups. In the headquarters building it is too easy to relax into the steady corporate nature of things. (Robert Franks, Senior Strategist, Telefonica O2 UK.)*

When Challenger Business Units within Establishment businesses don't work it is often because the parent becomes generally more preoccupied with efficiency than innovation.

> *In establishing the budget airline GO, British Airways had the possibility of a new alternative Challenger business. But instead of learning from it and encouraging innovation in the Estab-*

lishment operation they attempted to control it, standardise it and eventually sold it to their challenger competitor Easyjet. This standardisation took place as it often does through a subtle drift towards the centre rather than it being an overt and explicit move.

GO were set up as being separate from British Airways but they had BA non-execs on their Board who were subtly steering it back towards the operating model they were familiar with. After the initial separate set up, GO were encouraged to share the benefits of BA's greater purchasing power for fuel, and although this gave short-term benefits and made financial sense, it also eroded difference. GO were now beholden to BA's procurement practices, speed of decision-making etc.

8.2 Avoiding Fat, Dumb and Happy

Nobody in the company feels anything but pretty young and new, especially as we are up against so many well-established high street brands. We don't feel we have made it or that we are the Establishment by any means. We look at our Universe as being retail, not just online retail, so we look at our competitors' store offers and windows and not just their websites. This drives energy and a lack of complacency in the business. I can look at every sector and determine someone who is bigger than us that I want to challenge. Having said that ultimately we are as interested in focusing on creating new markets such as digital books as we are on competitors in current markets. (Brian McBride, CEO, Amazon UK.)

Something that helps successful Challengers is the ability to conceptualise change as emergent, continuous, ever present and flowing rather than a programmatic stop/start process. This is particularly helpful and testing in the moment that you think you have made it, especially when others are recognising your success and the new standards you are setting for competitors to follow. At that point, have you got it within yourself to open up again to the rigors of further discovery and exploration? Can you be proud of what you have achieved and light enough on your feet to give up any attachment to it?

Without this approach you end up lurching from one change to the next rather than continuously pushing the boundaries and surprising your customers and yourselves. In the Establishment way of thinking about change there are periods of intense action and awareness followed by a desired period of 'sustainability'. The longer the period of stability goes on the more out of date the organisation becomes until someone or something triggers the next round of change. Perversely this has the effect of exhausting an organisation over time as it always feels as though individuals are left catching up no matter how the change might be positioned.

> *While Innocent has been a Challenger brand for all of its existence, the past ten years, we now need to think about taking a different position as a Challenger to the next sector we want to take on. The risk is that we package up what we think consumers already know about us rather than being really committed to adopting a new stance in the sector. (Douglas Lamont, Director of Innovation, Innocent Drinks.)*
>
> *Pizza Express has always been a challenger - as the first "casual dining" restaurant, initially it*

challenged the very idea that eating out had to be stuffy and expensive (think candlesticks, prawn cocktail starters and dressing up to go out). But 45 years later, the norm of relaxed and reasonably priced eating out is well established. Therefore we have found it important to change the narrative of what we are challenging to remain true to the pioneering spirit of the brand and business. With our new narrative we focus on the promise of 'feeding great conversations', a new stance without losing our original belief system. (Emma Woods, Marketing Director, Pizza Express.)

8.3 Keeping Lean and Hungry

Some of the most successful Challengers have made a virtue out of paranoia. Andy Grove at Intel wrote a book called *Only the Paranoid Survive.* Steve Jobs at Apple talks a lot about being paranoid, as all great innovations will come from your competition. Whilst paranoia in its strictest sense has a quality of mistrust of others at its core it also has the quality of hypersensitivity to signals that something is different or changing in the environment. Even after achieving success, Challengers don't express their paranoia as a means of forbidding doubt or keeping out new points of view, they use it as a means of responding quickly to a competitive world that is constantly moving, shifting and changing around them.

A common means of building in discomfort and renewal to the Challenger organisation is to err on the side of under resourcing at all times. This creates a constant pressure within the system that brings with it energy, instability and learning.

When I first joined O2, I was immediately struck by the collaborative culture that the company's office fostered. Everyone was thrown together by virtue of the fact that there were more people crammed into a space that, at the time, was too small and slightly 'unpolished.' It just felt like the kind of environment where cost matters and getting things done right was the priority. Walking round to people's desks and collaborating was the essence of the culture and there was an atrium area that still exists today, where people would just sit down and talk – instead of booking rooms and having formal meetings. Most impressively the CEO's office was a modest room on the first floor office right next to the stairs where the door was constantly open. (Robert Franks, Senior Strategist, Telefonica O2 UK.)

Partnerships and collaborations offer another key means by which successful Challengers harness sources of rejuvenation that produce more internal disturbance despite historical achievement. Apple and Google have harnessed the collective power of an army of tiny little start-ups to drive their new software development. Despite having a well developed internal R&D capability Procter and Gamble have a 'connect and develop' initiative running, that targets 50% of their pipeline to be initiated outside their own business. GlaxoSmithKline and other pharmaceutical Challengers are increasingly reliant on external biotechnology discoveries from partners that are then internalised and aggressively developed.

Structural change is another means of staying lean and hungry internally; this can apply at both micro and macro levels. Structures and processes are often an inherent block to a Challenger Spirit thriving organisationally. Many successful Challengers realise a little too late that they have grown in a way that is destroying the culture of success they created in the first place.

> *Nokia the market leader in mobile handsets found it difficult to respond to the challengers such as Apple that were introducing smart phones. After taking too long to respond competitively, they finally decided in 2009 to split their original business unit into two, one for smart phones and the other for standard mobile phones.*[2]

> *In 1981 there was a big celebration at IBM because the Department of Justice that had pursued IBM and tried to break them up failed so they celebrated that they could keep everything together. If they had been broken up maybe there would not be a Microsoft today or a Dell or a SAP maybe others. So one remedy to keep a company young, agile is to break it up, which is almost impossible for those that have built it to comprehend. One remedy for a dominating force, GM, IBM, Kodak, break it up, make it smaller and create new Challengers. Breaking up AT&T produced South Western Bell, Lucent and Baby Bell. (Professor Herman Simon, Author of Hidden Champions of the 21st Century.)*

8.4 Becoming the Establishment

> *A question that I have pondered a great deal is "How do Challengers manage to hang on to their Challenger Spirit, particularly when they grow and taste success?" There are many organisations which start out as Challengers, somewhere along*

the way they begin to play safe and to lose their edge, sometimes they disappear altogether.

I have had some personal experience of leading an organisation through its struggle with this question; a struggle, which was ultimately unsuccessful. I cast my mind back to the early days of One2One which I was part of. It was the first digital mobile phone service to launch in the UK in 1993 and we were challenging the sector on many fronts – the technology had not been used before, the branding was very different, the pricing was innovative, our target market was new and had never been of interest to the incumbent mobile phone businesses. We had a confidence about what we were trying to achieve and a lively, vibrant spirit to go with it.

Personally, I was in a state of shock having joined One2One from the very epitome of the establishment... BT. I was astonished by the relative lack of process, lack of control, the freedom we had to choose the way we did things, the open disagreements and the fierce passion for the successful launch of the business. It felt to me like I had no safety net and boundaries. Far from this making me feel liberated it actually made me feel scared. Suddenly I felt very uncomfortable and anxious within this unpredictable environment. When I look back it makes me think of the accounts of the behaviour of battery chickens who are unwilling to leave their cages when liberated. Their need to stay within an environment that has been safe and familiar keeps them stuck where they are, even if it is much more unpleasant compared to the alternative being offered. As uncomfortable as it was I now see it as the kind of environment Challengers thrive in. Successful Challenger organisations are skilled at causing instability internally and externally and they know how to lead their businesses through the anxiety this causes.

Unfortunately, over time One2One lost the Challenger Spirit that had been such a key part of its successful beginning. How did we (One2One) manage to throw away the exciting and innovative culture that we had? How did we manage to become stuck and timid? What convinced us that control was so much more preferable to experimentation?

I think that a combination of factors worked together which allowed the Challenger Spirit in us to evaporate. Firstly, once the commercial launch of the business was complete we no longer had the clear purpose that had galvanised us. We were unable to create a new one that we really found compelling and simple. We became much more confused and fragmented in our opinions; our instability became tiresome rather than creative.

To make matters worse, Orange launched with similar aspirations to ours but a completely different level of ambition and resolution. We watched Orange create a true Challenger brand, with a Challenger spirit and a confidence in their actions that left no one in any doubt as to where they stood. They were very clear on what they were trying to cause and the purpose they were there for. They achieved pre-eminence in the market within a very short time, overtaking even the long established players Vodafone and Cellnet. We became much more attuned to watching them and trying to imitate them rather than sticking to our own course.

Thought leadership is such a vital part of being a Challenger in a sector and One2One lost its thought leadership to a competitor. Worse still it now tried to emulate the market leader's culture rather than hold onto its Challenger Spirit. I can remember the conversations that were common around One2One about needing to 'grow up' and our reverence for mature businesses. There was a real yearning not to be considered a child anymore and to have adult behaviour with its implications of self-control, predictability, process and discipline.

Our purpose became 'wanting to grow up'. I wonder why we wanted this so badly and why we were unable to see the benefits of a more childlike and creative state? Perhaps it allowed us to avoid the more difficult question of exploring what we wanted to be. As Orange grew up, it too lost its Challenger Spirit both on the outside in terms of their brand and, according to friends working there, on the inside in terms of their culture.

It seems to me that this is a mirror of the way we live our lives. We spend our childhood being encouraged by parents and the education system to 'grow up' and then we spend so much of our time as adults trying to re-discover what we had as children – spontaneity, wonder, excitement, honesty, joy, fun, uncertainty. In growing Challenger businesses we often repeat the same pattern. (Asher Rickayzen, Relume.)

8.5 You Have to Work at Growing Old Disgracefully!

Most of what is described in the previous sections of this chapter is the outer work of Growing Old Disgracefully. In common with previous chapters this outer work is impossible to do effectively without the corresponding inner work. This inner work is the fuel that ignites a wider and more idiosyncratic perspective, it literally keeps you on fire. The questions at the end of this chapter provide you with an opportunity to challenge your inner state more deeply.

At this stage of your Challenger journey you may need to change or add to some of the influences on your leadership so that you are thoroughly refreshed and not simply an incrementally different version of what has gone before.[3]

Could you create a peer-learning group with others who are at the same or at a more advanced stage of the journey? These groups at their best provide support and challenge to each other in order to be continually flexible in thinking, feeling and behaving.

What can you change in your personal habits and routines to shake things up a little? Change your communication style? Change your hairstyle? Change your dress code? Change how you get out of bed?!! Anything you can disrupt just for the sake of it, no matter how trivial this might seem; it changes neural pathways and will freshen up your Challenger thinking.

Many Challenger leaders find contemplative processes such as meditation a useful part of looking at the inner work more consciously. Other contemplative processes can include walking, swimming, singing, dancing, tai chi, cycling. Anything that challenges some of the social conditioning that constrains you and challenges the assumptions, beliefs and values that are part of your identity.

Keeping working on your ability to cause instability. The need for this pattern of behaviour can diminish as the Challenger starts to feel more successful but what you don't use becomes rusty. Keep practicing having difficult debates, difficult conversations and confrontations.

With success it might become easier to avoid your difficulties and fears but your ability to respond also benefits from continuing to face into them as quickly as you can, keeping your adrenergic system working and developed so that you respond as elegantly as possible. Work with the fears, don't resist them through unthinking fight, flight or freeze responses.

As Challengers become more successful and realise the positive effects of their own power they often feel drawn to change society in some way big or small. If you have this urge, do something, no matter how small it seems. It helps evolve your leadership in a significant way.

The rebel, subversive, temperate radical in your character will have been accessed as part of your Challenger success. It is worth checking back at this stage if the rebel has gone to sleep on the job and what it might take to reawaken him.

The end point of all this work can sometimes be a realisation that leadership for the next stage of the Challenger journey is better suited to someone other than yourself and that your energy, work and desire are needed elsewhere.

The Practice Ground

As Challengers we know that our time is now and we are responsible for what we do with it. That includes Challenger leaders who have had great success in the past. The past is only called up in our memories; there are still plenty of challenges to face into today and then the next 'today' and then the next 'today.' In sitting with a very successful Director recently a discussion surfaced about how to acquire more courage and overcome underlying personal fears, as he started to think about the next phase of his work and what would compel him. He was acutely aware that he was facing a choice that many of us also come to at a certain point in our careers. Namely can I rest in my success or break myself open again and become an adventurer another time? After a pause he asked 'how can I learn about courage and fear? No one here would believe I lack the one or have to deal with the other. I have become a very successful fish in this pond by challenging and leading; but I know there is more I could do if I just had more courage and less fear.'

In the spirit of the true Challenger and with the deep necessity to grow old disgracefully, this was our response to that question:

'Don't think that you can learn about courage and fear by reading more books. At this point in your life and given what you have accomplished you need to be more radical: physically take yourself to a place or a situation that causes you fear and fully encounter it, work with it and come along side it for a while. Tibetan Buddhists have a profound practice for working with fears that really seems to work. Whatever the fear is, they imagine it happening to them over and over again, they actually ask for more of it! If you fear being eaten by a crocodile in your dreams, in this practice you would stop running, turn around and invite the crocodile to bite you, then demand that it swallow more of you and then beg it to eat you whole! So if you fear ageing, boredom, poverty, illness, routine, insignificance, whatever strongly activates you, take yourself to it for real, witness it and come up close and personal to it. Get out there and seek it out. That is courage and that is the Challenger spirit!'

To grow old disgracefully is not the same as returning into the fold of the Establishment once you have achieved a certain level of success, even though the temptation to do this can be huge, particularly if you start to develop a mindset about what you 'deserve' and about taking it easy while others have their turn. We have seen some very promising Challengers appear to move through a typical curve of Challenger performance and perspective. Starting out young and passionate, hungry for change and sensitive to the deadening aspects of Establishment thinking, developing skills and making changes, which bring rewards, only to then see them then slump into a comfort zone of abundance and insularity.

Equally we have worked with Challengers who have developed their skills, caused great phase shifts and have gone on to mentor new Challengers or aspire to social action. They use their experience to creatively push and challenge the Establishments that exist all over the place through their accumulated wisdom in the autumn and evening of their lives. These people are not a spent force, they don’t rest on their material wealth and they don’t end up becoming part of the new Establishment. They continue their work; this is the way they have chosen to live their life, so what else could they do?

Getting Stuck In

Inner Work

- Distinguish a situation in which you have been holding on to your certainty or where you are strongly attached to what you have now achieved. What do these attachments provide for you? What might you be trying to avoid through these attachments?
- What are the messages you are picking up in your mind/ body telling you to move on?
- What frightens you about your future self?
- What would you never want to happen to you at work?
- What does aging mean to you and what is it an opportunity for as a challenger?
- What is the wildest and craziest thing you can do to stretch yourself?

Outer Work

- How is the Challenger narrative changing in your organisation? How will you tell the new story as compellingly as the old one?
- Where will your restlessness find its next focus? What are you pulled towards in terms of your future growth?
- What are you pulled towards in terms of how you could be of service to your organisation in the next phase? Is it different from the last phase?
- What will be your next trial or test? In what ways is it already present?

Your Notes, Insights and Scribbles

What Good Looks Like

Relentless in the pursuit of new achievements.

- An overpowering need to achieve and an unending hunger for success.
- Fuelled by fresh ambition.
- Never runs out of desire to go to new limits.
- Never satisfied with results.
- Doesn't rest on laurels.
- Always wants to achieve more.
- See the possibility to beat and exceed what has gone before.
- Measures self and the team against what could be and not what is.

Passionate about reinvention.

- A desire to be unique.
- A desire to set new standards.
- Remembers where they and the team / organisation have come from.
- Constantly looks for new breakthroughs.
- Seeks to redefine the team and organisation into more than the sum of its current parts.
- Continually creates imaginative new possibilities.

Has a radar for potential.

- Constantly examines the external environment for patterns and changes.

- Seeks personal learning from unconventional sources.
- Looks for opportunities not just in own market, but in other industries.
- Displays a healthy paranoia.
- Maintains an active external network looking for opportunities and possibilities.

Staying nimble.

- Doesn't accept the pressure of other people's expectations.
- Want to prove themselves again and again.
- Keeps the elation of winning and sense of achievement.
- Is eternally optimistic.
- Can change structures and processes quickly if they are proving to create limitations.

9 Keeping Yourself Honest

In an earlier chapter we explored the idea of the 'near enemy'. It is time to go back to this concept again and spend some time keeping ourselves honest.

The near enemy is a Buddhist concept that is designed to help us distinguish more closely when something is hitting the mark and when something looks similar but actually misses the point completely. These are the domains where we can fool ourselves. To complete this model, there is also the far enemy. Easier to spot because this tends to be the opposite of what you are trying to cause.

The near enemy of the Challenger spirit is the unwitting replacement of one Establishment orthodoxy with another that can be packaged into a formula and watered down. This is the shadow that Establishment thinking casts, and it has been doing this for so long that we are seduced into believing it is to be expected. Establishment organisations bring an approach to wisdom and novelty that turns each into a formula to be replicated. The former has spirit, emergence and experimentation; while the latter is really a bit fake.

If we are going to stay true in this endeavour we have to be able to spot the signs of the near enemy. If our inner state remains fundamentally attached to the way things are in the Establishment, all we can do is assume the role of a Challenger for the sake of looking good. The people in this book who have offered their experience to you are certainly not perfect, but they have all come to see that a fundamental reframing of their leadership is an aspiration worth fighting for. They know it is worth it for the thousands of people who are employed in business, for those of us who rely on their goods and services to ease or enrich our lives, for a society that benefits from their wealth generation and finally for themselves.

9.1 Witnessing the Establishment

Near enemy: Mirror, mirror on the wall, who is the fairest of them all?

The way to distort this pattern of behaviour is to put yourself too much into the centre of the activity. It is very easy to develop the skills of discernment and criticism of others and see how much needs to change around you. By doing that the tendency is to seek differentiation and comparison by seeing your own intentions or actions as somehow better or separate from what is going on around you. This is effectively partial witnessing and partial avoiding. Going deeper into the near enemy, it is also possible to miss the point of this practice by taking your already existing view of what needs to be done to change the situation and using this behaviour as an opportunity to simply impose your view. In this way you are falling into the trap of thinking that no one witnesses the Establishment like you do!

9.2 Purposeful Instability

Near enemy: Moving the deckchairs

You can really miss the mark on purposeful instability if you think that the point of it is really only to change or move things about. When you make this mistake, you may look like a Challenger but the quality of disturbance you actually facilitate is more in the nature of political nuisance than of creating an opening for the Challenger spirit to find its form. It is your ego that is likely to trip you up. When you are working firmly inside this pattern, your action is driven by the realisation that the frozen Establishment needs a deep shake to cause energy for change to surface. The corporate jargon of 'quick wins', 'salami slicing', and 'low hanging fruit' can often be part of the near enemy of Purposeful Instability. If you are driven by looking good then it is unlikely you will access, release and channel the levels of anxiety that are part of causing Purposeful Instability.

9.3 Hope and Ambition

Near enemy: Personal obsession

There are two important and mature aspects to the pattern of hope and ambition: firstly, maintaining a deep-seated aspiration that things will improve in the business, the second is that your ambition is expressed as a "we" rather than an "I" statement. Your ambition brings benefit to many and not just yourself.

A personal obsession is characterised by the meeting of your own needs, resolving your own dilemmas and satisfying your own desires but cleverly couched in language that makes it feel like a corporate narrative. If you are operating from this place your will and energy are likely to be affected more strongly by your own desire for personal achievement or avoidance of disappointment.

9.4 Challenger as Learner

Near enemy: Challenger as labeller

There is a very common shadow of this pattern of behaviour in large organisations where development opportunities have been readily available but also closely tied to personal advancement. This inevitably means learning becomes formulaic. Leaders do learn, but they mostly learn the language of fitting in. Some become exemplars of the theory of what they are supposed to be like. It becomes a game that is only really exposed when we are under pressure to embody what we purport to know about. If you do this for long enough, you can even begin to believe it yourself. Think of the leaders who can share the details of the theory of coaching, yet rarely adopt a coaching approach when their people are struggling.

9.5 Dance, Prod and Shuffle

Near enemy: Dance like a butterfly, sting like a bee

The near enemy of this persistent, balanced, kind and tenacious pattern of behaviour is really to be found in your intention. When you miss the mark it is likely to be because you desire to score a point, win an argument, expose a weakness in another, make yourself or your team look good or wear someone down to foster avoidant agreement. The intention behind any of these activities shows two things:

The first is that you, despite what you say, really believe that change is delivered by strength and power (namely yours), and the second is that you secretly still hanker for control but feel you must pretend not to.

The bee sting is very significant here. Leaving people smarting when you have danced around them is an indication that you have missed the mark with this credo. As Robert Aitkin Roshi says, "arrogance announces to the world that I do not feel at ease with myself".

9.6 Being the Face on the Dartboard

Near enemy: Being a martyr

We have covered some aspects of this near enemy in the chapter on this pattern of behaviour. However it is worth reminding us here that being a martyr is a very seductive and compelling situation when you as a Challenger leader slip into exhaustion or feeling unsupported.

When you get this pattern right the darts still land on you but you have a deeper well of resilience and a degree of wisdom to realise that you are simply the target of emerging anxiety. You have the wisdom of being able to see that you are both important and at the same time very ordinary. This is a crucial aspect of keeping yourself straight.

If you miss the mark and enter the territory of being the martyr, you are announcing to yourself and others that you have intensified beliefs about your own importance and significance. Once again your ego has popped up in a place where it really isn't needed!

9.7 Don't Despair!

Knowing what the near enemy for each of the patterns is can help you navigate a path towards creating a Challenger spirit and avoiding the pitfalls of your own shadow getting in the way. For every aspect of the patterns there is probably your own personal near enemy. As you get started you will find them; or rather as you get started they will find you. This is normal. In many ways when you are learning and feeling your way into a new way of leading, it is inevitable that you will sometimes miss the point.

10

Take Heart – an Eye on the Future

Over the years we have met many more defenders than Challengers, but it is the Challengers we remember, have been inspired by and have wanted to introduce to others. What marks these people out is not some higher intellect, or greater physical strength. They seem to have two defining characteristics. The first is the courage to overcome their fear. They test themselves through a series of demanding trials that challenge their spirit. Through these trials they create the second characteristic. The development of strongly held personal values and beliefs that are deeply meaningful personally and to those they lead. This is in contrast to the 'slogans' that many other leaders carry around, sounding good but feeling detached from them.

Challengers are in the business of transformation. Starting with themselves, their families, their teams, their businesses and ending ultimately with their society. This process of waking up is like seeing the lights go on inside ourselves. We love watching that and supporting it; what is more, we have to encourage it in us all, possibly from a much earlier age than we do currently.

If the next century is half as demanding as it appears to be from here then we are going to require as many of these lights as we can muster.

One of the most common metaphors used to describe transformation is that of the caterpillar turning into a butterfly. But that is only half the story and not necessarily the most interesting part! In certain insect larvae masses of hypodermic cells are carried inside the larvae in an undifferentiated way, until they begin to mature. At this point groups of these cells that appear the same as all of the others begin to mass into 'imaginal discs', and the process of differentiation begins. This process begins with a gentle dissolution of the larva in preparation for the maturing insect to emerge. The internal discs then actually create external novel structures that have been lacking in the larva such as eyes, legs, antennae and wings.

The seeds of gentle dissolution of the larvae are already present in Establishment organisations; they reside in the hearts of leaders who know that there is another way to think which is not contaminated by a pervading view of stability. If you work in an Establishment organisation do not make the mistake of believing that you are the only one who feels constrained, frustrated and sometimes bewildered. Creating 'imaginal discs' of potential requires you to connect with others, share your views, and do things to keep your collective will for change alive.

We propose that the Challenger patterns of behaviour presented here are the 'imaginal discs' of transformation for Challenger leaders. Stacking up together they give you the means to sense, see, wade through the trials facing you and use your wings to stay afloat. Doing the inner work on your leadership generates the outer manifestations and structures that are not visible at the beginning.

While we admire the Challengers in this book, we have never met a perfect one either. In fact, their imperfections often define them more than their capabilities. When beginning their processes even the least experienced or least confident of them had some of these inner 'cells' that were the foundations for novel skills or talents to emerge. All that was needed for their emergence was that they took the first step, facing their trials and overcoming their fear. As we said before, this is not a 'great man' theory; it is a method for all to participate in. To find your courage you have to know what you are frightened of. We all have it and actually it helps to guide us to deeper inquiries about what we need to be doing with our lives inside and outside organisations. Each of the Challengers we admire has decided to peer into the fear box and have a rummage around. They have discovered in doing that kind of inner work that they are more capable than they thought of taking on their own inner establishment. This maturing moment doesn't have to be big or public to be meaningful, to facilitate a dissolution of your fears so that you can touch your own Challenger spirit. What is important to know is that you are a possibility and you already contain the elements to differentiate yourself as a Challenger Leader.

Continue your work: if this is the way you have chosen to live your life then there will be nothing else you can do! Keep testing yourself. Your trials of strength are here to develop you as a Challenger and will be here for the rest of your life if you are willing to keep seeking them out. Go well. Khurshed Dehnugara & Claire Genkai Breeze 2011.

Afterword

I wish this book had been available to me early in my career. It lays out, far more lucidly than I ever could, everything it took me a lifetime in business to gradually recognise for myself, and then some.

It is not another 'how to' book. It's a thought-provoking book whose focus is that poorly charted territory between doing what you've always done the way you've always done it; and being able to create the circumstances in yourself, in your organisation and in those around you to resist the usual, to disrupt the status quo, to challenge the habits of years and cause meaningful, positive, lasting change.

In my long career in marketing and advertising, working with leading companies around the globe, I have had the privilege of working closely with a small number of Challenger leaders for whom this concept would be very familiar. Typically however, I more often worked with leaders who would be less likely to recognise it.

Challenger leaders are both brave and self aware. They know when an idea is tired, or when the way everyone has become used to looking at something is not how it really looks, and they know they have to challenge it.

Challengers have at least two key factors on their side. The first has to do with character, with self confidence, self awareness, independence of spirit. Given insight, these qualities can be cultivated and committed to, but they are qualities whose maturity depends on a whole variety of influences and experiences in our formative years and they come more naturally to some than to others.

In my experience many non-Challengers may well have it in them to become Challengers but their career path has been such that they are won over to the expected path and become champions of what they mistakenly see as 'the way we do things' or 'our corporate culture'. Ironically they often have had outwardly very successful careers. They will have been promoted frequently, and will have developed considerable loyalty to the organisation. But they will seldom entertain or try to explore a less usual path because they somehow deem it against the corporate ethos.

The second factor is perhaps a consequence of the first. All the Challengers I have known seemed to have some kind of internal compass to which they were true and on which they relied for courage and steadfastness of purpose.

I have seen them hold fast in the face of criticism from above and below, not obstinately or aggressively, but with quiet firmness. They have been prepared to resign rather than just go along; they have been ready to go back and start over rather than try to make the best of a failure; they have summoned the energy to relentlessly explain their point of view against repeated reservations; and they have typically quietly withdrawn once success was assured, happily spreading the credit while moving on to new challenges.

This book addresses closed minds, complacent minds, routine minds. It explores the spirit of challenging. It inspires us to look inside ourselves, inside our organisations, to think afresh, to see with new clarity, to find and strike out on the road less travelled. I expect it will come as a fascinating, provocative and quite possibly very profitable revelation.

Brian Harrison
ex Chairman
Dentsu Young & Rubicam, Japan

Notes

Introduction

[1] Doyle, Dane, Bernbach. (1962) *We Try Harder*. Campaign developed for Avis Rent A Car.

1. Challenger Spirit

[1, 2] Morgan, A. (1999) *Eating the Big Fish.* London: Wiley & Sons.

[3] Lowe, A. (2010) The Story is King, *Sunday Times* (July 4).

2. Witnessing the Establishment

[1] Worthen, B. (2009) Seeking Growth, Cisco Reroutes Decisions. *The Wall Street Journal* (August 6).

[2] Chang, S-J. (2008) *Sony Vs Samsung: The Inside Story of the Electronics Giants' Battle for Global Supremacy.* London: Wiley & Sons.

[3] WPP. (2005) *Annual Report and Accounts 2004,* London: WPP.

[4] Clark, N. (2010) Crozier Draws up Strategy to Make ITV 'Fit for Purpose'. *The Independent* (August 4).

[5] Mason, B. (1993) Towards Positions of Safe Uncertainty. *Human Systems: The Journal of Systemic Consultation & Management,* Vol. 4, 189-200.

[6] Siegel, D. (2007) The Mindful Brain: Reflection and Attunement in the Cultivation of Well Being. New York: W.W. Norton.

3. Purposeful Instability

[1] Branson, R. (2006) *Screw It Let's Do It.* London: Virgin Books.

[2] Sibun, J. (2008) Family Baker Warburtons Reaps the Dough. *Daily Telegraph* (July 20).

[3] Capell, K. (2009) Novartis: Radically Remaking its Drug Business. *Business Week* (June 11).

[4] Sutton, R. (2002) Why Innovation Happens when Happy People Fight. *Ivey Business Journal,* November/December.

[5] Heron, J. (1990) *Helping the Client.* London: Sage.

[6] Morgan, A. (1999) *Eating the Big Fish.* London: Wiley & Sons.

[7, 8, 9] Siegel, D. (2007) The Mindful Brain: Reflection and Attunement in the Cultivation of Well Being. New York: W.W. Norton.

4. Hope and Ambition

[1] Morgan, A. (1999) *Eating the Big Fish.* London: Wiley & Sons.

[2] Senge, P., Otto Scharmer, C., Jaworski, J., and Flowers, B. (2004) *Presence: Human Purpose and the Field of the Future.* London: Nicholas Brealey Publishing.

[3] Wieden and Kennedy. (2004) 'what if Honda?' *A Submission for The Marketing Society Awards 2004.* London: Wieden and Kennedy.

[4, 5, 6] Senge, P., Otto Scharmer, C., Jaworski, J., and Flowers, B. (2004) *Presence: Human Purpose and the Field of the Future.* London: Nicholas Brealey Publishing.

5. Challenger as Learner

[1] Morgan, A. (1999) *Eating the Big Fish.* London: Wiley & Sons.

[2] Lowe, A. (2010) The Story is King, *Sunday Times.* (July 4).

[3, 4, 5] Begley, S. (2009) *The Plastic Mind.* London: Constable & Robinson.

6. Dance, Prod and Shuffle

[1] Berfield, S. (2009) Starbucks: Howard Schultz vs Howard Schultz, *Business Week.* (August 6).

[2] Cremer, J. (2009) *Improv: Enjoy Life and Success with the Power of Yes.* Oxford: Sunmakers.

[3] Johnstone, K. (1981) *Impro: Improvisation and the Theatre.* London: Routledge.

7. Being the Face on the Dartboard

[1] Guthrie, J. (2009) Man in the News: James Dyson, *Financial Times.* (October 16).

[2] Kramer, P. (2005) *Against Depression.* New York: Viking Press.

[3] Stewart, I., Joines, V. (1987) *TA Today a New Introduction to Transactional Analysis.* Leicester: Lifespace Publishing.

[4] Leith, L., Miller-Karas, E. (2010) Trauma Resiliency Model, *www.traumareourceinstitute.com.*

8. Growing old Disgracefully

[1] Morgan, A. (1999) *Eating the Big Fish.* London: Wiley & Sons.

[2] Parker, P. (2009) Nokia to Split up Mobile Devices Unit, *Financial Times.* (October 17).

[3] Gregory, J. (2009) In Conversation, *www.josiegregory.co.uk.*

Illustration Credit

I was delighted to have been invited to illustrate "Challenger Spirit". The prospect both scared and excited me. I scoped out a plan for each section and began working through it, trusting the overall concept would come. About a month before the submission deadline, what I describe as 'the magic' happened, as it always does in the creative process. It came in the shape of the Frog in the Box. I knew instantly it represented a strong, exciting concept, so different from what I had been doing so far, that it would mean starting again, this time with much more energy and excitement.

My inspiration for the images came originally from Henry Moore's war art; powerful sketches with an ethereal quality that had led me some time ago, to want to experiment with combining photography with drawings. The Frog in a Box was the first of these to emerge.

I have to thank Kim Foster, who sketched both the frog and the street runner; and Khurshed and Claire, for giving me the opportunity.

Karen Foster